THE FEDERALISTS VS.
THE JEFFERSONIAN REPUBLICANS

THE FEDERALISTS VS. THE JEFFERSONIAN REPUBLICANS

Edited by **PAUL GOODMAN**
University of California, Davis

HOLT, RINEHART AND WINSTON

New York • Chicago • San Francisco • Atlanta
Dallas • Montreal • Toronto • London

CONTENTS

INTRODUCTION

It would be hard to imagine how Americans could govern themselves without political parties constantly vying for the voters' support by formulating alternative policies and offering different leaders to deal with the vital public business. Yet these institutions for democratic decision-making did not exist at the birth of the Republic. Those who designed the federal constitution in 1788 made no provision for parties and, indeed, the founding fathers unceasingly denounced groups seeking political power as "factions"—scheming, narrow, selfish elements pursuing goals contrary to the common good, the bane of all experiments in free government.

Nevertheless, in the decade immediately following the adoption of the federal constitution, the first precursors of modern political parties began to appear in the United States. For over a decade, the Federalists and Jeffersonian Republicans vigorously competed for power. Federalist dominance during the 1790s generated a strong Republican counterattack that captured the national government in 1801 and steadily overcame opposition in the states.

Rarely has partisan conflict engendered so much fear, hatred, and bitterness as in the 1790s. Each party accused the other of desiring to subvert the established order and of harboring dangerous partiality for foreign nations and alien ideologies. Each denounced the other as factious and challenged the legitimacy of opposition. It seemed for a while that the worst fears of the framers of the constitution were being realized: the nation was torn apart by corrosive rivalries that were destroying the unity indispensable for national survival.

But by 1815 the prospects had brightened. The young Republic had survived the transfer of power from Federalists to Republicans in 1801 without experiencing disorder, and it had fought Great Britain a second time to defend its sovereignty. Firmly established, it was independent, free, and prosperous. Political parties, which none had anticipated and all had deplored, were a principal means by which Americans made government sensitive to the various sentiments and interests in the nation; they enabled citizens to settle differences peacefully and helped forge a resilient national unity that withstood passionate rivalries without sacrificing freedom or diversity.

Despite the critical role parties have played in translating the Constitution

1

into a workable instrument of government, historians have been unable to agree on their precise origins, their impact, or the reasons for the decline of the first two-party system after Jefferson's election in 1800. For a long time American history was written without much understanding of the complex social forces that lay behind election campaigns, party rhetoric, and prominent political personalities. In the early years of the twentieth century, a new generation of historians, many of them sympathetic to the reform impulses of the Progressive period, discovered that the struggle in their own day between the overprivileged and the underprivileged had roots deep in the American past. Differences in kinds and amounts of property, they believed, always generated rival economic interests, or "classes," which persistently sought power to advance their own well-being, usually at the expense of others.

Charles A. Beard was the most influential exponent of an economic interpretation of American history. For him it unlocked the secret of the origin of American political parties, a development explored in the first group of selections. Beard argues in the initial selection that perennial rivalry between "conservative" merchants, manufacturers, capitalists, and other large property owners and "radical" mechanics, workers, planters, and small farmers shaped American political experience. It accounted for social conflicts, including the battle over ratification of the federal Constitution as well as the ensuing party struggles, which gave new form to continuing conflicts. Those "radicals" who opposed the Constitution because they believed it served the interests of the wealthy became Jeffersonian Republicans, while "conservative" supporters of the Constitution sought to reap the rewards of their earlier victory under the Federalist banner. For a decade Federalists ruled, according to Beard, for the benefit of merchants, manufacturers, and holders of public securities until the rural masses, led by large planters, organized the Republican party as a vehicle for recapturing government from the "moneyed aristocracy." Success came in the "revolution of 1800" when Thomas Jefferson, the philosopher and champion of agrarian democracy, was elected President. Thereafter, rival classes fought for power through the instrument of the party system. Inasmuch as Beard thought that class conflict was a constant in American politics, one wonders how well it explains contemporary political divisions between Democrats and Republicans.

For a long time Beard's forceful account went unquestioned. Then historians began to re-examine critically its fundamental assumptions. In the second selection, William N. Chambers searches through the experience of the country's formative years to discover how young nations today might achieve political stability and still remain democratic. The early American parties, Chambers argues, were innovations of the first magnitude. Rejecting the conventional loose use of the term "party" to describe almost any kind of political organization, Chambers insists that the parties emerging in the 1790s were unique institutions unlike any that existed earlier in America or elsewhere. If parties did not derive from continuing class conflicts, as Beard thought, but from new conditions stemming from the tasks of nation building under the federal constitution, one must specify precisely what functions parties performed and by what means they discharged them.

Whereas Chambers explores the process of political modernization in one country, Robert R. Palmer in the next selection places American party development within the larger context of democratization occurring throughout the Western world toward the end of the eighteenth century. Despite their desire for isolation from the turmoil in the Old World, Americans could not remain aloof once the French Revolution unleashed vast social changes in Europe. Some became "Gallomen," others "Anglomen." Palmer's examination of the impact of the French Revolution on American politics suggests that it divided Americans more sharply than any other event in the 1790s. Despite the widespread desire for peace, the country came perilously close to war first with England and then with France, as Federalists and Republicans violently disagreed over the conduct of foreign affairs. For both parties, the fate of the young Republic hinged on the outcome of the revolutionary struggles abroad. An important question students must try to answer is why some Americans became pro-French and Republicans and others pro-British and Federalists. Can either Beard or Chambers account for the saliency of the French Revolution in American politics?

The intensity with which Americans reacted to events abroad may be explained by re-examining the social sources of party support. The final selection on party origins by Paul Goodman analyses the groups from which the parties drew strength and for whom they spoke in the large and important state of Massachusetts. Goodman challenges the fundamental assumption of Beard, widely shared by other historians, that groups such as farmers, merchants, planters, and artisans formed homogeneous classes with common interests and unified political loyalties. He argues that economic groups were highly complex and often deeply divided; not all farmers or merchants had identical interests or agreed on the best ways to advance them. Nor can differences among occupational groups entirely account for all the fissures in society which fed party rivalry. Religious, ethnic, geographical, and status rivalries also generated social tensions on which parties thrived.

However one explains party origins, the two rival formations expressed differing philosophies of government. These are examined in the next group of selections. It is rare that in one generation there are so many extraordinary public men as the leaders of the first parties—Washington, Hamilton, Adams, Jefferson, Madison, and Gallatin, to name a few. Though Washington was the titular head of the Federalist party, the first Secretary of the Treasury, Alexander Hamilton, was its chief architect, a one-man brain trust, master propagandist, and tireless backstairs manipulator and tactician. The selection by Clinton Rossiter analyzes Hamilton's basic beliefs and helps to explain some of his strengths and weaknesses as a party leader and at the same time reveals the presuppositions of an important stratum of American society for whom Hamilton spoke. Though Hamilton is usually depicted as a political realist, his attempt to bind capitalist groups to the new government by appealing to their economic interests was coupled with an expectation that less favored groups would cheerfully acquiesce in arrangements which he believed advanced the general welfare. Such an assumption seems inconsistent with Hamilton's view of man's selfishness and of the harsh realities of practical politics. Perhaps Hamilton thought that the majority would defer to an elite whose virtue, wisdom, and competence in governing entitled them to lead. If so, Hamilton and other Federalists were disappointed, and one must try to explain why their expectations proved delusive.

Though Jefferson was the leader of the Republican party, he worked in close partnership with his fellow Virginian, James Madison. Madison was the counterpart of Hamilton, a man of ideas, an intellectual in politics, but also a tough polemicist and party organizer. His fundamental views on government differed sharply from Hamilton's, as the next selection by Adrienne Koch demonstrates. What are the chief points of conflict between Hamilton's and Madison's ideologies? Why did Madison's ideas find a broader and more sympathetic audience than did Hamilton's? Despite their differences, the two men played similar roles as formulators and expounders of their parties' basic doctrines.

As Federalists and Jeffersonians developed leadership, cadres, sources of popular support, and ideologies, they also adopted new political practices, one of the consequences of party development examined in the next group of selections. At first, political organizations lacked legitimacy, because Americans were accustomed to think of them as factions subverting the common good. However, to increase their effectiveness, the parties came to develop permanent organizations that would unite the faithful and periodically mobilize the electorate. Carl E. Prince in the next selection describes the development of a political machine in New Jersey, a prototype of organizations emerging elsewhere, which utilized the partisan distribution of lucrative offices to build a corps of loyal activists who operated the new party machinery. Prince also sheds further light on the types of people who became Jeffersonian Republicans. How does his description of the kinds of people who became Republicans compare with Beard's and Goodman's?

Another consequence of party growth was expansion of the suffrage. In the next selection, J. R. Pole shows how this came about in Maryland, where it was less the result of the belief by either party that a more liberal franchise was a good thing than the unforeseen outcome of party rivalry and maneuvering for immediate advantage. Pole's account of the attitudes of Maryland Republicans toward widening the suffrage makes one wonder how democratic "Jeffersonian Democracy" really was. Moreover, does nearly universal white male suffrage in itself mean that politics were democratic?

Parties not only expanded the suffrage and built political organization but they also promoted greater equality of economic opportunity. In the next se- lection, Bray Hammond examines the relationship between banks and politics, explaining further the consequences of party development. The Republicans are usually pictured as the party of agrarian democracy, the enemy of Federalist fin- anciers, speculators, bankers, and other members of the "paper aristocracy" whose wealth stemmed from the manipulation of paper values rather than from hard work. Jeffersonians singled out for attack the First Bank of the United States as an instrument by which a moneyed aristocracy acquired special privileges from government and undue influence that threatened the survival of republican gov- ernment. Yet, according to Hammond, after Republicans acquired political power, more new banks proliferated than ever before. To resolve this paradox, one might argue that Republicans were simply opportunists who liked banks they controlled and disliked those they did not. Or perhaps Republicans were divided among themselves over the desirability of banks, with the entrepreneurial minded favorably disposed, while the less ambitious and enterprising were suspi- cious and critical. Have historians been misled because they ascribe the anti-bank convictions of a few outspoken leaders and party philosophers to the heteroge- neous coalition that comprised the Republican formation? Thus Jefferson is usually depicted as the champion of the yeomen farmers even though his party came to dominate the leading urban communities of the young Republic.

However one resolves this dilemma, partisan rivalry over the distribution of charters incorporating banks helped to transform the nature of the corporation. Republicans found themselves excluded from most of the early banks, which were usually Federalist dominated, and when Jeffersonians obtained power, they promptly voted themselves valuable new charters. In this way, party rivalry ex- erted pressures that helped to make the acquisition of corporate charters a right readily available to enterprising citizens instead of a privilege monopolized by a few.

The first party system proved fragile. After their defeat in 1800, the Federal- ists never again won control of the national government and even many of their state strongholds crumbled. Meanwhile, the Republicans were becoming such a heterogeneous collection of forces, infiltrated by ex-Federalists, that they lost the distinctive qualities that had sharply differentiated them from the opposition. By the 1820s, the first parties had dissolved and new ones were emerging.

Unable to agree on the reasons for the development of parties, historians are equally unable to agree on the reasons for their decay, as the final group of selec- tions illustrates. First, Stephen G. Kurtz examines the closing years of Federalist dominance in the late 1790s to find the sources of subsequent defeats. Kurtz fo- cuses on the deadly split between Adams Federalists and Hamiltonian Federalists which deprived the party of the unity essential for victory in 1800 and survival thereafter. But why did the party fatally split apart? And why didn't the ex- periences of being a minority force Federalists to unite after 1800?

Arguing that the Federalists' difficulties were rooted in their ideology, Shaw Livermore in the next selection suggests that the party's fundamental beliefs were outdated relics of an earlier aristocratic age, increasingly irrelevant in a society undergoing democratization. Yet one wonders whether large, slave-owning planters in the South who were often Republicans were much more sympathetic to democracy than were wealthy Federalist merchants and financiers? What were the essential differences, if any, between the attitudes toward democracy of Republicans such as Madison and Federalists such as Hamilton? And how do these distinctions reflect differences in the constituencies represented by the two parties? Even if one accepts Livermore's contention that Federalist views were unpopular, one has to explain why the party did not adjust its principles to regain public favor after it lost elections.

In the final selection, Noble E. Cunningham, Jr., helps to explain Federalist decline by exploring the sources of Republican success. One key to Republican victory was a powerful party organization that helped to keep the party in office. Unlike Kurtz's Federalists who were sharply divided among themselves, the Republicans achieved and maintained a high degree of unity. And unlike Livermore's Federalists who were out of tune with public opinion, the Republicans fashioned a political philosophy and program, according to Cunningham, which captured the popular imagination.

Another fruitful way to explain why the first American party system declined is to determine the necessary preconditions for party development, as suggested in the first group of selections, and then to inquire if these prevailed after 1800 and if not, why not. The reasons why parties first arose in the United States in the 1790s, what their consequences were, how party ideologies differed, and why the early parties disappeared are not simply interesting puzzles to bemuse students of history. The United States is the oldest republic in the world because an earlier generation, unwilling to accept the conventional wisdom of the day which held that no large, diverse republic could long survive, formulated fresh ideas and invented new institutions to overcome the obstacles that threatened the success of republican government. None of these innovations was more important than the political parties; through them a numerous and heterogeneous people, scattered across a huge continent, governed themselves by resolving differences peacefully and adjusting to the forces of change in an orderly, democratic manner.

In the reprinted selections footnotes appearing in the original sources have in general been omitted unless they contribute to the argument or better understanding of the selection.

CHARLES A. BEARD (1874-1948), the most important
American historian of his generation, formulated and
popularized an economic interpretation of American
history that remains highly controversial. Over eleven
million copies of his books were published, including
The Rise of American Civilization (1927), an account of
American history that exerted a strong influence a
generation ago. Beard believed that differences in the
kinds and amounts of property created rival classes
whose economic interests clashed. The political behavior
of farmers, workers, and businessmen, Beard argues, was
an expression of class interest; each group sought power
to advance its own well-being, even at the expense of
another's. In the following selection, Beard explains the
origins of political parties in the young republic as the
result of class conflict.°

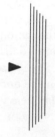

Class Conflict and
the Rise of Parties

It is customary to separate American
political history into three periods, using
changes in party names as the basis of the
division. According to this scheme, there
have been three great party alignments
since the formation of the Constitution:
Federalists against Republicans (1789-
1816), Whigs against Democrats (1830-
1856), and Republicans against Democrats (1856 to the present time). Although
the dates are merely approximate,
they furnish useful chronological clues.

But this division is arbitrary and only
for convenience. In fact, there has been
no sharp break in the sources of party
strength, in policy, or in opinion. On the
contrary, these three alignments have
been merely phases of one unbroken conflict originating in the age of George
Washington and continuing without in-
terruption to our own time.

The first of these alignments—Federalists against Republicans—was connected
more or less directly with the contest over
the framing and adoption of the federal
Constitution.[1]

[1] The roots of party antagonism lie deep in colonial times. In Virginia, there were contests
between the upland farmers and the gentlemen
planters of the seaboard before the seventeenth
century closed. During the stirring prelude to the

Authorities are generally agreed that the main support for the Constitution came from merchants, manufacturers, government bond holders, and other people of substantial property interests "along the line of the seaboard towns and populous regions." They are likewise agreed that the opposition came mainly from the inland farmers, debtors, and less prosperous sections of the country.

The feelings aroused by the contest over the Constitution had not disappeared when the first administration was organized in 1789 with Washington as President and friends of the new system installed in all branches of the government—executive, legislative and judicial. With Alexander Hamilton, first Secretary of the Treasury, in the lead, the advocates of the new order, soon to be known as Federalists, carried through a series of economic measures which in time divided the country into two powerful parties. In summary form, these measures were as follows:

1. The funding of the national debt. All the old bonds, certificates, and other evidences of indebtedness issued by the Continental Congress during the Revolution were called in and new bonds for face value given to the holders.

2. The assumption of the revolutionary debts of the states. The federal government also called in the revolutionary debts of the states and issued new federal bonds instead; that is, the federal government assumed the obligations of the

Revolution against Great Britain, the division between the Patriots and the Tories was supplemented by sharp divisions among the former. More than once the mechanics of the towns frightened the merchants by radical demands and serious rioting. All through the War of Independence, the revolutionists were split into radical and conservative factions—mechanics and poor farmers against the merchants and possessors of large property. See Beard, Rise of American Civilization, Vol. I, pp. 266-68

states and added them to the general debt of the nation.

These two operations, funding and assumption, deeply affected the purses of classes and masses. Before Hamilton began his work, the old bonds and notes issued during the Revolution had been selling at from ten to twenty cents on the dollar, because the national government and several states had failed to meet their obligations. During the dark days of uncertainty, a large part of this paper had been bought by speculators from the original holders at low prices with a view to profit taking. In the end, funding and assumption increased the value of the depreciated securities to the amount of approximately forty million dollars—a huge sum for those days. To raise the money to pay the interest on the debt, the federal government had to lay heavy taxes on the people, most of whom were farmers, not bondholders.

3. Protective tariff. The third measure on the Federalist program was the protection of American industries by the imposition of customs duties on imports coming into competition with American products. Hamilton openly favored an elaborate system of protection. Although his plans were not adopted in full, the first revenue bill passed in 1789 was mildly protective and, in time, other protective features were added.

4. The United States Bank. Under Hamilton's leadership, Congress chartered a banking corporation, authorized it to raise a large capital composed, three-fourths, of new federal bonds, and empowered it to issue currency and do a general banking business.

5. A sound national currency. Under the new Constitution, the states had to stop issuing paper money. The gold and silver coin of the United States now provided by law became the money of the

country, with the notes of the United States Bank circulating on a parity.

6. Discrimination in favor of American shipping. To encourage the construction of an American merchant marine, Congress provided that the tonnage duties on foreign-built and foreign-owned ships should be five times as high as the duties on American ships. In line with this, other concessions were made to native shipping, especially that engaged in the China trade.

7. National defense. In creating a navy and a standing army, Congress had more in mind than the mere defense of the country against foreign foes. The navy was useful in protecting commerce on the high seas and the army in suppressing uprisings such as had occurred in Massachusetts in 1786. In other words, economic factors as well as patriotism were involved in the process.

8. Foreign affairs. When the wars of the French Revolution broke out in Europe, the Washington administration, largely inspired by Hamilton, frankly sympathized with England as against France and looked on the contest in the Old World as a conflict between property and order on the one side and democracy and anarchy on the other— akin in fact to the political dispute at home.

Now these measures were not excursions in theory. They were acts of power involving the pocketbooks of groups, affecting the distribution of wealth and the weight of classes in politics. Certainly the first six of them bore directly upon the economic interests of the citizens.

Under these laws, large sums of money were paid to the holders of government bonds who had been receiving little or nothing; people who were moderately well off one day found themselves rich the next. Under these laws, stockholders in the United States Bank earned hand-

some profits on their investment, protected manufacturers entered upon a period of prosperity, and merchants and money lenders were enabled, by the sound currency system and adequate judicial assistance, to carry on their operations safely in all parts of the country. Under these laws, heavy taxes were collected to pay the interest on the bonds and to maintain the new government.

Were these things done for beneficiaries at the expense of other classes, notably the farmers, or did the increased production caused by the operations more than cover the cost? On this point economists disagree and the historian cannot answer the question mathematically.

At all events, however, a considerable portion of the American people came to the conclusion that the Federalist measures and policies above enumerated in fact transferred money to investors, merchants, manufacturers, and the capitalistic interests in general, at the expense of the masses—a majority of whom were farmers and planters. "This plan of a National Bank is calculated to benefit a small part of the United States, the mercantile interest only; the farmers, the yeomanry, will derive no advantage from it," complained a member of Congress from Georgia. The protective tariff on steel will operate "as an oppressive, though indirect, tax upon agriculture," lamented a Congressman from Virginia. "The funding system was intended to effect what the Bank was contrived to accelerate: 1. Accumulation of great wealth in a few hands. 2. A political moneyed engine," protested another Virginia statesman.

In time, the citizens who took this view of the Hamiltonian program were marshalled, first as Anti-Federalists and later as Republicans, under the leadership of Thomas Jefferson, who was by occupation and opinion well fitted for his mission. A planter, Jefferson was acquainted with the interests of agriculture. Moreover, he believed and said openly that "cultivators of the earth are the most valuable citizens. They are the most vigorous, the most independent, the most virtuous, and they are tied to their country and wedded to its liberty and interests by the most lasting bonds." In logical relation, he had a low opinion of commerce and industry, which created urban masses. "The mobs of great cities," he asserted, "add just so much to the support of pure government as sores do to the strength of the human body."

Holding such opinions, Jefferson set out to enlist a large following in his struggle against the capitalistic measures of Hamilton. He made his strongest appeal directly to the agriculturalists of the country. And when his party was fully organized he took pride in saying that "the whole landed interest is republican," that is, lined up on his side of the contest.

Speaking of the Federalists arrayed against him on the other side, Jefferson said that they included all the federal office holders, "all who want to be officers, all timid men who prefer the calm of despotism to the boisterous sea of liberty, British merchants and Americans trading on British capitals, speculators and holders in the banks and public funds, a contrivance invented for the purposes of corruption."

Appealing to the farmers and the masses in general against the larger capitalistic interests, Jefferson's party inevitably took a popular, that is, a democratic turn. This was in keeping with his theories, for he thought that kings, clergy, nobles, and other ruling classes of Europe had filled their countries with poverty and misery and kept the world in turmoil with useless wars. The common people, he reasoned, if given liberty and let alone, would be happier under their own government than under any ruling class.

To their economic arguments, the Jeffersonians added a constitutional theory. They declared that the Constitution did not give Congress the power to charter a bank, provide protection for manufacturers, and pass certain other measures sponsored by the Federalists. This was a "strict construction" of the Constitution; that is, the powers of Congress were to be interpreted narrowly and the rights of the states liberally. Although the Federalists included in their ranks most of the leading men who had made the Constitution, they were thus accused of violating the very fundamental law which they had conceived and adopted. In this way, arose the wordy battle over the "true meaning" of the Constitution and the "rights of states" which occupies such a large place in the history of American political loquacity.

To the disputes over domestic questions were added differences of opinion about foreign policies. . . .

The more radical elements of the population, fresh from their own triumph over George III, remembered with satisfaction the execution of Charles I by their ancestors, and took advantage of the occasion to rejoice in the death of another ruler—the French monarch. A climax came in 1793, when France called on the United States to fulfill the terms of the treaty of 1778, in return for the assistance which had been given to the Americans in their struggle with England. The radicals wanted to aid France, either openly or secretly, in her war on England, but Washington and his conservative supporters refused to be drawn into the European controversy. So the Americans were divided into contending groups over foreign policy, and the division ran in the main along the line already cut by the

Federalist-Republican contest over domestic questions.

As the critics of the administration, known at first as Anti-Federalists, slowly changed from a mere opposition group into a regular party and took on the name Republican, the friends of the administration with Hamilton, John Jay, and John Adams in the lead, began to organize for political warfare under the banner of Federalism. In the third presidential election, the party alignment was complete. Jefferson, the leader of the Republicans, was roundly denounced as an atheist and leveler; while Adams, the Federalist candidate, was condemned by his opponents as "the monarchist." So sharply drawn was the contest that Adams was chosen by the narrow margin of three electoral votes.

During Adams' administration, the Federalist party was thoroughly discredited. The Republican newspapers heaped indiscriminate abuse upon the head of the President and the Federalists generally. As a result Congress pushed through the Alien and Sedition Acts—the first authorizing the President to expel certain aliens deemed dangerous to the safety and peace of the country, and the second making the publication of attacks on any branch of the federal government a crime.

Under the Sedition Act, many Republicans were severely punished for trivial criticisms of the administration. For example, Callender, a friend of Jefferson, was convicted for saying, among other things: "Mr. Adams has only completed the scene of ignominy which Mr. Washington began." In letter and spirit the Act seemed contrary to the amendment to the federal Constitution guaranteeing freedom of press and speech against federal interference. At all events,

the two laws called forth the famous Kentucky and Virginia Resolutions, and convinced even those moderately inclined towards democracy that Federalism meant the establishment of political tyranny. The death knell of the Federalist party was rung. Jefferson was elected in 1800 by a substantial majority over the Federalist candidate.

It has been the fashion to ascribe to the Federalists a political philosophy born of innate ill-will for the people. "Your people, sir," Hamilton is supposed to have said, "is a great beast"—as if in a burst of petulance.

Now this imputation is not entirely just. No doubt some of the emotions to which Federalists gave free vent were the feelings common to persons of large property—feelings of superiority and virtue. But there were practical grounds for distrusting "the people." Throughout the Revolution "the lower orders" had given trouble to the right wing of patriotism, threatening to upset the new ship of state before it was launched. Indeed, some blood had been shed in conflicts among the Patriots themselves before independence was won.

To the Tories who remained in America and rallied to the Federalist cause, the masses were, of course, contemptible in opinion and conduct. In the eyes of the Patriots of the right, the new democracy was responsible for the failure to pay the interest on the national and state debts between 1783 and 1789, for the refusal to grant aid and protection to American industry, for the uprising against the "rich and well-born" in Massachusetts in 1786, and for sundry other disturbances in the body politic. When, therefore, Federalists cursed the people—as they did in gross and in detail—they were not merely expressing a conservative temper. Rather were they reasoning, so they thought, from experience, bitter realistic experience at that.

For twenty-eight years, from 1801 to 1829, Presidents calling themselves Republican occupied the White House—Jefferson, Madison, Monroe, and John Quincy Adams—and except for a short time at the beginning they were well supported in Congress by party members of their own persuasion. During this period, the Federalist party, as a national organization, died a lingering death. It continued to put up candidates until 1816, but after that failure it disappeared from the national theater. Deprived of a shelter all their own, active Federalists then went into the Republican organization and did what they could to bend it in their direction, while the intransigents of the old generation often sulked in their tents, lamenting the evil days upon which they had fallen.

Although they possessed the power of government, the Republicans, it must be said, did not have a perfectly free hand in carrying their policies into effect. For more than half of this period, the nations of Europe were engaged in the devastating Napoleonic wars which interfered with the shipment of American agricultural produce to Europe, and for a brief term the United States was at war with Great Britain. Owing to foreign events beyond their control, the Republicans were compelled to adopt many devices not to their liking, or at least contrary to their professions.

Nothing had caused more discussion among the Republicans than the national debt. Members of the extreme left had argued that it should be repudiated, that inasmuch as soldiers had given their lives to the revolutionary cause property owners should sacrifice their financial contributions. Not many, of course, held this extreme opinion, but some did, and the Federalists had attributed such views to the Republicans in general. A middle faction of Republicans opposed repudiation but thought that some reduction should be made in the generous terms adopted by Hamilton. All Republicans agreed that, in any case, the debt was a burden on the taxpayers, most of whom were farmers, that it was a source of speculation and corruption in Congress, and that it should be discharged in full as soon as possible.

Hence the Republicans paid off the national debt as fast as they could, and they were in a fair way to extinguish it when they got into a war with Great Britain in 1812 and were simply forced to increase it.

Hamilton's second great political institution, the United States Bank, likewise came in for its full share of Republican attack. On this point there was no compromise. In 1811, at the end of the twenty-year term, the charter of the Bank expired, and the Republicans refused to renew the life of the great "money power." The banking business passed into the hands of banks chartered by the states and the paper notes of these concerns flooded the country, some of them good, many of them bad.

If it had not been for a crisis, the Republicans probably would have stood firmly against any revival of the United States Bank. But during the war with Great Britain, which they undertook against the wishes of the business and commercial sections, they were driven into a corner in their efforts to pay their bills. In the end, they had to choose between surrendering to the private banks, which had sprung up in the business centers such as Boston, New York, and Philadelphia, and establishing a semi-political government bank under their own control. In the dilemma, they naturally chose the latter plan; in 1816 a Republican Congress chartered the second United States Bank and a Republican President approved it. Members on the left wing opposed this action and in growing numbers waged war on the new "money power." As we shall see, they split the party and destroyed the Bank. Even members of the middle and right factions accepted the Bank as a measure of necessity merely to save the government in their hands from a worse fate.

Into the tax program of the Republicans, the War of 1812 broke with incredible force. They had bitterly opposed the Federalists' direct taxes, which fell heavily upon land, and their internal taxes, especially the tax on whiskey which reached into the pockets of thousands of farmers who had little stills of their own. Once installed in office, the Republicans reduced and abolished until they cut the direct and internal revenue taxes and duties down almost to the vanishing point. These burdens so odious to agriculture had nearly disappeared when several of them had to be revived after war was declared on Great Britain. Wars cost money and somebody must pay for them! Yet it could be truly said that, until necessity compelled them to choose another course, the Republican statesmen had done their best to ease the taxes distasteful to their agricultural constituents.

Tariff schedules likewise became involved in war necessities. Those established under Federalist auspices were mildly protectionist in character. Hamilton's thorough-going program had been rejected by Congress. As the rates which the Republicans found in force on coming into office were light and yielded large revenues to pay off the hated debt, no radical changes were made in a downward direction.

On the contrary, the opposite happened. The wars in Europe, the War of 1812, the blockades, and the depredations played havoc with American farmers and planters. Unable to ship their produce abroad freely, they found it spoiling on their hands or sinking in price for the want of a market. Why not have a home market, therefore, beyond the reach of wars? Manufacturers approved the idea and offered to furnish the market for the produce of farms and plantations if they could get sufficient protection against foreign competition.

Despite loud protests on the left wing, the Republicans adopted in 1816 a protective tariff bill which would have delighted Hamilton had he been alive to see it. In a long oration, John C. Calhoun, a South Carolina planter, defended the bill in Congress on the ground that it would furnish a market for the produce of the soil. And the stoutest opposition came from New England whose shipping interests, engaged in a lucrative carrying trade, did not want foreign imports reduced by high tariffs. The business was economic but tables were reversed. As we shall see, when conditions changed, planters and farmers could alter their tariff policies. At no time did they forget to cherish the land.

Land—the source of Jefferson's party interest—also figured in two other strokes of policy made by the Republicans during this period. In 1803 they purchased the Louisiana Territory from Napoleon and thus added enough land to satisfy, it seemed, farmers and planters for a century or more. True to their class, the financial and commercial Federalists on the seaboard opposed the purchase on the ground that it would soon enable the agricultural interests of the South and West to dominate the country. That dominance was exactly what the Republicans wanted and, as they had a majority in Congress, the treaty of purchase was ratified.

The question of land similarly entered the War of 1812. According to the usual school-book traditions, this war was fought in defense of American rights against British depredations on the sea, but Professor Julius W. Pratt, in his *Expansionists of 1812*, has demolished that theory. Commercial interests were generally opposed to the war. Planters and farmers voted for it. The grand outcome was to be the annexation of the two Floridas for the planters and the annexation of Canada for the farmers. In the process, the Indian allies of Great Britain on the frontier were to be reduced to order so that pioneers could take up their abode in peace on the edges of American civilization. Owing to inadequate military preparations the plans failed.

The truth is that the Republicans did not believe in a powerful navy and a powerful standing army. In Jefferson's eyes, a navy was a costly Federalist device for which farmers and planters had to pay in taxes simply to protect the property of American shippers on the high seas.

Loyal to farmer traditions, Jefferson feared a strong regular army. It was expensive, he thought, and unnecessary because the popular militia could be relied upon to keep order and defend the country. Although Jefferson used the navy with vigor and telling effect on the Barbary pirates, he and his party reduced rather than strengthened the regular armed forces of the country. The failure to achieve their ends in the War of 1812 may be laid at their door. Farmers did not realize that banking and fighting were professions that could not be learned overnight.

On the whole, it could be said that the Republicans were loyal to the landed interest which they frankly championed in politics. Most of their apparent veerings in the Federalist direction were due to that loyalty rather than to any conversion of heart.

In the development of political theory, the Republicans proceeded with considerable directness.

On the side of ceremony, their task was easy. For various reasons the Federalists had wanted to surround the government with pomp and circumstance. Many of them were old Tories who had enjoyed prostrating themselves before the monarchy and the church in the days of King George. Some of them were rich and idle, and could not think of anything more diverting than presidential balls, receptions, and etiquette. Others, taking a more utilitarian view, looked upon parades, lace, gold braid, brass buttons, spangles, horse hair, and robes as useful things to awe "the mob," give it respect for government, and keep it on its knees. Since a number of Jefferson's followers were among the people called "the mob" by Federalists and since farmers did not as a rule care for ceremony, the Republicans laid great stress on simplicity and abandoned many of the ceremonial precedents set by Washington and Adams. Jefferson once stopped at a boarding house and walked to the capitol for his inauguration! "Jeffersonian simplicity" was a great slogan for succeeding generations, even though Jefferson lived lavishly most of his life.

This doctrine of simplicity, in fact, fitted well into the larger Jeffersonian creed of "the less government the better"—a creed likewise adapted to the primitive agricultural life of the country. Lest there be some doubt about his political philosophy on this score, Jefferson was careful to make a full statement in his very first inaugural. Besides praising religious liberty, majority rule, freedom of press, "the encouragement of agriculture and of commerce as its handmaid," the diffusion of information, and the "supremacy of the civil over the military authority," Jefferson clearly described his political ideal: "a wise and frugal Government which shall restrain men from injuring one another, shall leave them otherwise free to regulate their own pursuits of industry and improvement and shall not take from the mouth of labor the bread it has earned. This is the sum of good government and this is necessary to close the circle of our felicities." In a word, here is the whole gospel of *laissez faire*, no government in business, so appropriate to simple agriculture, and, half a century later, as a curious fate would have it, to the requirements of manufacturers in resisting factory legislation.

With a similar pertinence to reality, the Republicans championed intellectual freedom. They had suffered severely at the hands of the Federalists under the Sedition Act, and they refused, when in power, to make use of the instrumentality they had previously condemned, until slavery—the labor basis of the planting system—was menaced by agitation.

In harmony with their general theories, but also resting on practical grounds, was the Republican creed respecting the judiciary. Believing in majority rule, Jefferson held that it was absurd and contrary to the Constitution to give to the federal judiciary the right to declare acts of Congress null and void, that is, as he put it, the right to prescribe rules for the government of the legislative and executive branches.

Beyond theory lay realities. A Federalist justice of the Supreme Court, Samuel Chase, had been particularly active in denouncing from the bench "dangerous democratic doctrines," and

the Republicans attempted to oust him by impeachment. Defeated in this effort by the Senate, they were all the more convinced in their opposition to what has been called "judicial supremacy." If they showed any tendency to relax, they were likely to be aroused again by a ringing decision against state rights by Chief Justice Marshall, a doughty Federalist whom the Federalists put on the bench for life just as Jefferson came to power for a term.

Only on one important point of political theory did the Republicans reverse themselves in practice. When they were opposing Hamilton's economic program, they held that the Constitution should be strictly construed, that the federal government could not do anything which the Constitution did not clearly authorize. However, when they came to exercising power themselves they were not seriously troubled by such strait-laced views. The Constitution certainly did not say anything about buying more territory; yet the Republicans bought Louisiana with great rejoicing. Jefferson thought the transaction unconstitutional, but lawyers found a warrant for it in the clause giving the President and Senate the right to make treaties. In any case, it took a liberal eye to find it.

With equal facility the Federalists, once loose constructionists, now that tables were turned, took a strict view of the Constitution. Since they were in the opposition, nearly everything Republican was "unconstitutional"—the embargo, the Louisiana Purchase, and conscription for the War of 1812, for example. If their speeches are to be taken literally, they were in great distress lest the Constitution be violated by the free interpretation made by Republicans.

Reviewing this reversal of political theory by both parties, a cynic might say that circumstances alter opinions and laugh softly at the constitutional eloquence of lawyers. But a fairer judgment would be that actions which we approve never appear in the same light as actions which we dislike. At all events, "strict interpretation" received a severe jolt at the hands of its authors and never wore the same aspect again.

If the Republicans grew a bit "loose" in their constitutional theories while they were in power, they at least contributed one fairly definite article of political faith, namely, the idea that no President should serve more than two terms. Washington had declined a third term—not because he thought it unconstitutional or contrary to political wisdom. The fact was that he had served his country for many long years and was in need of a well-earned rest. Jefferson was also thoroughly weary in 1809 and did not want a third term on any conditions, but he made a kind of philosophy out of his preference, saying: "General Washington set the example of voluntary retirement after eight years. I shall follow it. And a few more precedents will oppose the obstacle of habit to anyone after awhile who shall endeavor to extend his term. Perhaps it will beget a disposition to establish it by an amendment of the Constitution."

Rustic simplicity, *laissez faire*, freedom of opinion, a critical attitude toward the judiciary, a strict but convenient interpretation of the Constitution, and the third term doctrine—such were the chief political articles among the professions of Jeffersonian Republicans.

Challenging Beard's view that the party conflict in the 1790s developed from the continuous struggle among classes, **WILLIAM N. CHAMBERS** of Washington University (1916-), maintains that parties were new institutions born of the needs of a fledgling nation confronting serious challenges to its survival. Like many contemporary social scientists, Chambers is interested in the process by which colonial regions become nations and how they can achieve stability and prosperity without resorting to totalitarian methods. Since the United States was the first new nation in modern history, the experiences of its formative years shed light on the process of nation building. In the following selection, Chambers delineates the role political parties played in this process in the 1790s, arguing that the new national government established in 1789 stimulated institutional innovation because pre-party methods of managing public affairs were no longer appropriate.°

Nation Building and the Rise of Parties

In 1790 Alexander Hamilton, as Secretary of the Treasury in the new government of the United States, proposed to Congress the first in a long series of measures aimed at the economic development of the new nation. Before he was finished he had brought into being a powerful political engine to advance his program, to support his determined effort to shape the destiny of the infant republic. In effect, he had founded the Federalist party. He began this task fourteen years after the declaration of American independence, seven years after the treaty of peace which followed the Revolutionary War.

In 1797 Thomas Jefferson boarded a coach at Monticello, the gracious home he had built on a Virginia hilltop. After three years of retirement devoted mainly to agricultural experiments and to country life, he was on his way to the nation's capital to assume fresh duties as Vice-President. Yet the trip of a week or so was more than just a return to the chores of office. It was a crucial stage in a political odyssey which was to bring him at last to full acceptance of active leadership in the opposition Republican party, a political force which was unique for its time.

The two events symbolize the genesis and ultimate establishment of national political parties on the American scene. These political engines were not only the first parties to adventure on the precarious ground of politics in an emerging nation but also the first true parties of modern times, appearing well before such formations developed in England or other European countries. They were shaped slowly and painstakingly, as part of a general progress in which the American states moved from colonial dependence and revolutionary uncertainties to become a stable, democratic, modern republic. Like the nation itself, parties were the work not only of Hamilton and Jefferson, and of other great leaders like George Washington, the industrious James Madison, and the conscientious John Adams, but of nameless lesser workers as well. The final result was not only parties but a system of competing parties in interaction. Yet no man could have said in advance just what the outcome would be.

Indeed, the whole national and party progress was beset by the difficulties and hesitations of exploration. It was fortunate that most of the new nation's leaders were men not only of high public faith and national vision, but of a profoundly pragmatic ability to learn and invent as they went along.

If parties were to act as unifying forces in the diversity of the nation, they had to prevail over thorny obstacles in the social and political structure itself.

The most obvious difficulty lay in the fact that the "nation" at the outset was actually a loose assemblage of thirteen states. Each had its own history, sense of identity, and political climate; and neighboring states were often engaged in intense rivalries. One of the aims of the Constitution of 1789 was to reduce such rivalries and join the states into a nation. Yet, even after the adoption of the new

frame of government, localisms persisted and a tangle of conflicting interests and attitudes remained within the states and across the country. Here were small-freehold farmers and great planters owning platoons of slaves; domestic merchants, shipowners looking to the trade of the ocean seas, and shipbuilders on the coastal streams; struggling manufacturers seeking home markets, and importers and exporters; and artisans or "mechanics." Here also were varieties of ethnic shoots and religious flowerings; divisions between sober "Anglomen" who adhered to English ways as the measure of stability, or sanguine "Gallomen" who saw the French Revolution as the millennium for the rights of man; and cleavage between men who wanted an "aristocratic," consolidated republic, and others who looked toward a "democratic" regime and state rights. In short, the nation was the scene of an indigenous, deeply rooted, conflicting pluralism. In the early American states, the multiform interests, sentiments, and opinions of this pluralism had produced a highly uncertain faction politics of hybrid combinations and perishable alliances. Furthermore, each state had its own taproots of power and its own government offices to fill, and thus its different leaders "ambitiously contending," as Madison put it, for preferment.

To bring the order of national parties out of such diversity was obviously no moment's task. This was particularly the case when scattered settlement, great distances, and poor roads impeded assembly and communication. In view of the fact that a truly national political arena first opened with the joining of the several states into the national government under the new Constitution in 1789, the political task looms as even more formidable. The surprising thing was not that America's political founders took so long to evolve parties, but that they managed to bring any order into the nation's politics at all. The process by which they did so was inevitably erratic and halting. It was also inevitably accompanied by much groping, by fumbling invention as well as brilliant innovation, and by doubts and reversals.

Indeed, American party founders scarcely realized at the outset that they were building parties. They did not see themselves as a set of political contractors who had undertaken to create a modern party system, and in any case they had no earlier plans or models to go by. In England, the mother country and chief source of early American practices, politics in the eighteenth century was still a helter-skelter of personal maneuvering and personal "connexions"—in the old spelling and the old style—of ties based on family, narrow bonds of special interest, or friendship. Public affairs were managed by a few aristocrats, great magnates, eminent families, dependent agents of the Crown, or occasional freebooters. The right to vote was limited to a thin layer of the population; it was common talk that many voting districts were in some Lord's or magnate's "pocket"; the mass of the people counted for little in political calculations; and governments could be made or unmade without regard to broad popular opinion. Despite the persistence of loosely applied labels like Whig or Tory, which actually denoted general persuasions rather than distinct political formations, there were no parties in the proper or modern sense. Furthermore, American politics in colonial times duplicated English modes in many ways. Thus, neither the English experience nor early American politics offered blueprints for the eventual development of parties.

Yet new forces were beginning to appear on the American scene, forces which as time passed stimulated new methods. Most American leaders of the Revolutionary era did want to establish a stable republic, more or less based on the popular consent which the Declaration of Independence in 1776 had promised. During the colonial years the right to vote had been accorded to many men who held a parcel of land; and the suffrage was extended during the Revolution or in the decade that followed to the point where American, as contrasted with English, political leaders were beginning to have a substantial electorate to deal with. Thus even in colonial times, Washington as a candidate for the House of Burgesses in Virginia had found it necessary to arrange for an appetizing outlay of rum, punch, wine, cider-royal, and beer to please the varied tastes and win the votes of electors in his district. . . .

In short, leaders faced with new ranks of voters had for some time been groping toward effective methods of popular appeal and toward native patterns of coordination.

By and large, however, such methods had remained fairly primitive and were in any case not employed by parties as such. In state after state in the American republic until the 1790's, politics remained a gamble of individual endeavor, or of shifting factions; of family cliques in New York, which virtually duplicated the patterns of old-Whig "connexions" in England, or of intermittent caucuses in New England; of social elites like the ruling "Fifty Families" in Maryland, or of exclusive "juntos" in much of the South. The slow evolution of political methods to deal with an expanding electorate was merely a foreshadowing of party practices, not the advent of true party action.

Additional obstacles to party development came from doubts about the wisdom of parties. For men like Washington or Hamilton, such doubts were concentrated around the question of the legitimacy of an opposition party. A man of forceful presence, a balancing and unifying force in politics, and the supreme hero of the Revolutionary War, Washington was convinced that once the new national government had been put in his hands, it was up to him and his chosen aids to manage it. Filled with determination to join the struggling states into a great and powerful nation, a farseeing leader of determined purpose, Hamilton also was impatient with criticism, intolerant of democratic demands or the very idea of opposition. Many other leaders held similar views. Uncertainties as to the wisdom of party went beyond fear of opposition, however, and were particularly apparent in the course of Jefferson himself. As easy and amiable as Hamilton was intense, Jefferson had won undying fame as the chief author of the Declaration of Independence and was also something of a practical visionary in politics, and his democratic vision of the national destiny usually ran contrary to Hamilton's view. Yet, although he has been hailed as the founder of the Republican party, he was in fact long unconvinced of the advisability of party action. . . .

. . .As late as 1797, the magisterial Washington in his Farewell Address voiced a still significant (if by then declining) view when he warned against "the baneful effects of the spirit of party generally," which he saw as serving "always to distract the public councils and enfeeble the public administration"—it was "a spirit not to be encouraged." The conception that an "in" party of those who held government authority should accept a stable party of opposition was slow to take hold. To many Americans, efforts toward an articulate "out" party of criti-

cism vying for power seemed to portend fires of disruption, if not the flames of sedition.

In short, the very idea of party rivalry was long suspect. In the retrospect of peaceful American party development it is easy to argue that the fear of party rivalry was exaggerated in the years of party formation, but it was widespread at the time.

Other conditions, however, were more favorable for the development of parties. In large part these followed from the special nature of the American Revolution, the way in which the new nation found its identity and established its character thereafter, and the political tradition and political system it began to evolve in consequence.

The American Revolution was a genuinely anti-colonial movement. It threw off, by violence, the ties of imperial control from London and ultimately established the thirteen colonies as legally independent entities joined in a new confederation. Many later emerging nations, however, have tended to look for inspiration more to the French Revolution of 1789 or the Russian Revolution of 1917 than to the American experience. For them, the striving for nationhood has been a long and bitter experience, a rebellion against foreign economic exploitation and foreign cultural domination as well as against foreign political control. For them, the national revolution has tended also to be a social revolution, as the French and Russian revolutions were. Like these revolutions, it has tended to bring sharp social cleavages, ideological animosities in an intense and sweeping anti-colonialism, and the hatreds toward old masters which accompany such overturns. The American rebellion was not a profound social revolution in this sense, although local "Loyalist" elites were displaced from power by American "Patriots," and the Revolution did inspire a decade of moderate reform. In this respect, the first great colonial revolt of modern times differed from many twentieth-century national movements. . . .

In part because their Revolution was not a social revolution setting system against system, class against class, or modern against fixed and traditionalist ways on the domestic scene, Americans were able to arrive more readily than many other new nations at basic understandings on political structure, at the same time that they were arriving at a consensus on political means. Much of the emerging national outlook was summarized in the Declaration of 1776 and the Constitution of 1789, and this outlook eventually became a tradition. It countenanced substantial freedom of action in the political as well as in other realms, and over the years this basic liberal view did much to reduce the fear of parties and even of opposition parties. The first amendment to the national Constitution provided clearly for freedom of speech, assembly, publication, and petition, and the rule won ultimate acceptance. The national tradition, growing in a favorable soil in which most citizens owned at least some measure of property and in which distinctions of rich and poor were minimized, also promoted an increasing degree of social equality and political democracy, along with attitudes that kept political conflict generally within a moderate range and subject to peaceful resolution. Fear of opposition or an opposition party remained for some time, but a counter-tradition could be invoked against it. Furthermore, intolerance of opposition reinforced by an official ideology could not be invoked as a revolutionary virtue.

Still, modern parties and the party system in the United States were indeed products of a labor of Hercules, and not "natural," untended flowerings from the soil of independence and popular government. Rather, parties were ingeniously shaped "artifacts," in the sense of structures built up over years by the industrious, if often groping, activities of men. To assume that a democratic political party system in the United States in the 1790's—or in any new nation—could grow overnight from independence and a democratic constitution, or be struck off at a blow by one or two great leaders, is to underestimate the problems involved. Revolution on Monday, independence on Tuesday, a Constitution on Wednesday, political parties on Thursday, orderly elections on Friday, stable democratic government by Saturday, and rest on Sunday—any such conception of political creation is the stuff of dreams. If parties and democratic party systems are the products of human ingenuity, time and energy in abundance must go into their making.

In the process of party building, American founders confronted and effectively solved a long series of political problems. Some were foreseen and some unforeseen, some were at hand from the outset and some emerged only in the course of the work. It was throughout an endeavor of pragmatic adaptation and inventiveness under necessity, guided at the beginning by immediate purposes or a general desire to prove the republican experiment, informed only later by a conception of party as a goal. The problems of establishing the republic and of establishing party overlapped, and in a sense they all involved the practical fulfillment of the national and democratic promise of the Declaration of Independence.

The first task was to fix workable patterns of legitimacy and authority in the new polity, under which the conflict of interests and opinions could go on within a larger national unity. The solution to this problem ultimately drew on elements as disparate as Washington's personal appeal and Jefferson's rationalist philosophy. As any emerging nation must, young America faced the issue of shaping national economic development and policy, with all of its payoffs and costs for different interests. As a new national power, it also faced the trying problem of establishing national identity and effective independence in an often threatening and sometimes contemptuous world. The first great, controversial steps in economic policy were taken by Hamilton, whose party found its origins in the ties of interest and action his program brought forth. Contention over world politics and foreign policy followed, pitting Madison against Washington as well as Hamilton, and Jefferson against Adams; and full-scale party division ensued. Yet policy was evolved, and the nation survived.

To man the posts of government and the new force of party, new recruits for leadership were necessary; and the nation was fortunate in the skill and imagination of the political lieutenants, cadremen and foot soldiers who came forward to administer public affairs and develop party-formations.

One task such men confronted was devising stable methods which could link a hitherto unprecedented mass public and electorate to hitherto unprecedented party structures. Another was forging sufficient unity within parties in government to enable them to govern coherently and bridge the gap between the constitutionally separated executive and legislative branches in the American system. The first great essay at governmental management was Hamilton's, and he accomplished much toward coherent policy. Within a decade, however, Jefferson and his co-workers had gone even further and achieved a near model of responsible democratic party government in office.

Given the pluralism and state-by-state fragmentation of power in the American federal system, party builders had to assemble national parties out of varied and widely scattered state and local materials. Indeed, the interplay (and often conflict) between disparate state and local elements on one hand, and national structures and concerns on the other, has been a continuing theme of American party development and action. After some years, the Republicans also developed modern organization to reinforce party strength, but the Federalists never arrived at this device.

With the establishment of parties, Americans faced the intricate problems of conducting a system of parties in competition and the delicate questions of accord in the idea of opposition and of the peaceful transfer of power from one party to another.

The eventual solution of these various problems was to become the story of America's formative political years.

American party development also touched another issue of fundamental concern. This was the question of the practical functioning of a democratic political system as a whole. Various processes have been proposed as the criteria of democracy: free entry to the political arena; widespread participation in the political system; effective representation for and balancing of varied interests in the society; open discussion and debate; free elections; government that is somehow responsive or responsible to the demands or judgments of the public or electorate; or the right to criticize government decisions. It is easy to speak broadly, as Jefferson did in the Declaration of 1776, of governments "deriving their just powers from the consent of the governed." It is more difficult in practice to realize such consent and to assure the faithfulness of governments to the governed, to meet significant criteria of democratic functioning. In practical terms, some sort of party system has proved necessary to the operation of modern democratic politics. . . .

In the process of nation building, the American founders explored many problems generic to new nations. Their experience cannot provide literal lessons for other peoples today, who face different conditions and must devise political procedures that are appropriate to their own circumstances, as their American predecessors did. Yet there are important parallels. The American instance revealed the significance of a concern for political as well as economic development in the progress of a new nation, as it also showed that political construction is bound to be difficult and disappointing to utopian hopes, and proved the value of moderate and pragmatic approaches to political problems. It brought to light important factors which may make for national stability, underscored the role of economic development as a foundation for democracy, and underscored the crucial role of broad as well as specialized education for promoting democracy and training leaders. It also provided an early example of parties as vehicles to contain the forces of pluralism and bring coherence into public policy. It demonstrated the eventual utility of a two-party system as an instrument of democracy and a device to redress imbalances of privilege and power. Finally, the American experience set a pattern for a responsible opposition which avoided the intransigence that may disrupt a nation. In short, it uncovered viable democratic ways to conduct the conflict of politics and manage government within national unity.

Yet at the time, no one could foresee the result. Only after they had taken long steps toward the solution of the political problems they faced, only after the tasks of party development had been accomplished, could American leaders and the American public look back and see what they had achieved. . . .

"As a general marches at the head of his troops," wrote Alexander Hamilton in his Memorandum Book, "so ought wise politicians, if I dare use the expression, to march at the head of affairs: insomuch that they ought not to wait the event, to know what measures to take; but the measures which they have taken, ought to produce the event." The maxim was copied from Demosthenes. It admirably expressed the political style of the arrogant but brilliant gentleman from New York who became the young nation's first Treasury secretary, promptly stepped forth as a bold, innovative policy advocate, and drew new issues. . . .

In his advocacy, political management, and nation building, Hamilton brought together the elements that came to constitute the Federalist party. He did not consciously set out to do so, but such was the ultimate result.

It took some time to set the government going, first briefly in New York and then after 1790 in Philadelphia as temporary capitals. The first session of Congress was devoted mainly to establishing the executive departments and the judicial branch, and to other housewarming chores. It was not until 1790 and 1791 that Hamilton presented his proposals, and a new political era opened.

His recommendations drew consistency from his basic politico-economic perspectives. They constituted what amounted to a comprehensive plan for the economic advancement of the new America, but one which was founded on the fact that the nation was already relatively developed economically, and which looked to powerful groups that development had brought forward. In brief, Hamilton sought a happy and fruitful marriage between the special interests of "moneyed men," and the larger interests of orderly national government, from which the one might derive strength and authority, and the other gain. An Anglophile, he admired the hierarchical political order he saw in Great Britain, and its elitist, ministerial style of government; to foster the marriage of wealth and government in America, he would copy the English model as far as he could. At the outset he called for the "funding" and "assumption" of the Revolutionary debts. By "funding," securities of the old Confederation which had depreciated sharply in the market would be exchanged at face value for interest-bearing bonds of the new government. By "assumption," the Federal government would make itself responsible for debts incurred by the states during the Revolutionary War. Next Hamilton urged Congress to charter a hybrid public and private Bank of the United States, which would hold federal funds and handle government financial transactions, meanwhile undertaking private banking, credit-extension, and note-issue functions. Finally, he proposed internal excise taxes as a means of raising revenue to sustain his debt policies, and a protective tariff on manufactured goods.

These proposals offered gratification to a wide range of interests, but this was not their only significance. The debt policies, for example, marked an immediate gain estimated at $40,000,000 for holders of public securities or speculators—"stock-jobbers," Jefferson called them at one point. A medley of other groups, from merchants or "infant" manufacturers to certain segments of agriculture or working men, could take satisfaction in other meas-

ures. Yet the farseeing Hamilton was not merely responding to group demands or playing broker to various interests. In particular, his fiscal proposals were by no means policies that were taken for granted even in the new American business community. As advocate and manager, he was rather staking a course of creative policy-making, and offering a coherent program, a sweeping, intricately devised program, which went well beyond the limited purposes of an old-style faction or the agenda of a caucus or junto. It was something the narrow political formations of previous decades could scarcely have envisioned, the sort of endeavor which has come to characterize parties at their best, as they have presented comprehensive formulations of public policy. Furthermore, Hamilton's policies were designed to have a wide appeal. Besides providing a payoff in economic development for business groups, his program as he saw it would stimulate national growth, increase the flow of goods and services, and raise living standards for the nation as a whole. In short, while Hamilton knew the need to recruit immediate political support from particular groups, he was also concerned that his policies promote a broad conception of the national interest—again, of course, as he saw it. At the same time, he was determined to prove that the new government could be effective, at least in economic rewards.

In this effort, he was favored by an unusual political context. Not only did he move in the protective shadow of Washington's prestige. He was also able to "produce the event" so brilliantly at the outset—only in the tariff did he fall much short of his goals—largely because he could "march at the head of affairs" along comparatively open ways. In a new governmental system still being formed and in an unstructured national politics, he found ready opportunity for his purposes.

At the outset, the legislative branch Hamilton addressed was a leaderless herd. Composed almost entirely of "Federalists," in the sense of men who had supported the Constitution of 1787, Congress set no direction of its own for the new government. During the first session of April-September 1789, in a nearly free flow of legislative individualism, members had agreed or disagreed as issues came and went. There was sharp cleavage over proposals by Vice-President Adams to establish a "high-toned" government by giving grandiose titles to the president and other such devices, but alignments on the issue disappeared with the defeat of Adams's proposals. The choleric "Billy" Maclay of Pennsylvania, an Ishmael in the Senate who smelled conspiracy in any alliance however temporary, noted periodic instances of "caballing and meeting of members in knots." Yet even he could find little consistency beyond certain joint exertions by the "mercantile interest," or the support that Pennsylvania, New Jersey, Maryland, and Delaware members gave proposals for imports to encourage manufactures, or the tendency of "the New England men" to join together in opposing molasses duties. The ramblings of individual views and shifting relationships were only occasionally joined into blocs representing particular interests or sections. Otherwise, there were not even clear factional divisions. A summary comment by Maclay on early Congressional behavior was not far from the mark: "The mariner's compass has thiry-two points; the political one, perhaps has many hundreds."

The sessions of 1790 and 1791, however, revealed the stamp of Hamilton's firm leadership. The law creating the Treasury Department had sketched unusual ties between the head of that department and Congress in the reports and interchange of information it required. Beginning with the debt-assumption issue, Hamilton elaborated these formal ties into the bonds of informal executive-legislative leadership, utilizing, in Maclay's phrase, "every kind of management." His "reports" were calls to action, and he and his assistants provided arguments and statistics for Congressional debates. He followed legislative affairs with the utmost care, keeping a sharp eye on timing, favorable committee appointments, and chances for maneuver. He met privately with members, and discreetly arranged informal conferences to draw his followers together. Everything "is prearranged by Hamilton and his group," Maclay cried in the anguish of opposition.

Although Maclay exaggerated, he was right in perceiving that the debt and bank issues, with the prestige of Washington's "name," had produced a "court faction." Its genesis in Hamilton's executive or "ministerial" leadership marked the beginnings of coherence and order in politics in the new nation's capital.

The emergence of management at the capital brought strong responses across the country. In the process, what began as a capital faction soon became a national faction and then, finally, the new Federalist party.

From the national center, ties of common interest and action were extended into the states, counties, and towns. Again Hamilton played a prominent role, weaving a web of correspondents out of his wartime associates, his business connections and friends, and the many individuals whom, as Secretary, he was able to oblige. His personal contacts and personal influence were used to draw

together a new political formation, which
eventually became less personal. The
Federalists also drew on the first American veteran's association, the Society of
the Cincinnati, a strongly knit organization of Revolutionary War officers and
their descendants. Such notable figures as
Fisher Ames and Theodore Sedgwick in
Massachusetts, John Jay and Rufus King
in New York, John Marshall in Virginia,
or Robert Goodloe Harper in South
Carolina joined the cause, along with
many others. Thus Hamilton's original
faction reached out into the countryside
and developed into a national political
structure which could support its capital
leadership by undertaking the labors of
propaganda, electioneering, and other
political tasks. Its key local leaders were
men of position and high respectability in
their communities: former military officers everywhere, or mercantile magnates
in New York; the Congregational divines
in Massachusetts and Connecticut, or
Episcopalian ministers in the Middle Atlantic region and in the coastal plains of
the South; captains of finance in Philadelphia, or great planters in Maryland
or South Carolina. From the Federalists'
center at the capital to their periphery in
the counties and towns, relationships
among established notables provided the
strong strands of the emerging Federalist
structure. Such notables drew in other
participants, and together they soon
formed the ranks of the active workers or
"cadre" of the emerging party.

Yet the party-in-the-making also rested
on a broad combination of interests and
opinions. Like any open major party in a
pluralistic society, it came to include in its
following a substantial range and significant density of groups and individuals.
Domestic merchants, men in the shipping
trade and shipbuilders, holders of public
debt securities, bankers, investors and fin-

anciers generally, owners of struggling
manufactories, great Tidewater planters,
dependent business and professional
men—all could look happily to Hamilton's promotion of enterprise under
the protection of government action.
Furthermore, most of these groups had
already enjoyed sufficient economic development to enable them to support their
interests with significant political power.
Yet the Federalist appeal was not limited
to capitalist or proprietary interests. Many
wage earners, particularly in shipbuilding
along the coastal rivers, where a man
might farm part of the time and work in
the shipyards another part, could see
employment and higher wages in Hamilton's proposals. Modest farmers who
looked to the export market could also
anticipate prosperity and higher prices as
a result of Federalist policy, although ultimately the great weakness in the Federalist fabric proved to be an insensitivity
to the concerns of agriculture as a whole.
The assumption scheme had a strong
appeal in states that had incurred heavy
Revolutionary debts and failed to pay
them off. This special issue operated in
Hamilton's favor in debt-ridden South
Carolina as well as in mercantile New
England. Indeed, Massachusetts and
South Carolina became the early
Northern and Southern foundations of
Federalist strength.

Their emerging structure and broad
base gave the Federalists a position of effective influence in the electoral arena.
Working through their network of notables and lesser leaders, and through
Hamilton's web of correspondents, beneficiaries, and officeholders, the Federalists
were able to put forward candidates and
mobilize voters for them. Though they
tended to look upon elections largely as
opportunities for the public to ratify their
policies, Federalist managers knew that

co-ordinated action in election contests was essential to maintaining power. . . .

The Federalists' achievement of full party status came with the development of emotional attachment to the party as such. The concerns of interest, economic as in Hamilton's proposals or otherwise, provided critical strands for party formation; but something more was also necessary. This was the emergence of unifying faiths and loyalties, of exclusive and distinctive "in-group" attitudes, of emotional commitments, of at least the beginnings of an ideology. Here again the charisma of Washington, his aura as a providential agent of national independence and national identity, supplied "an *Aegis very essential*" to Federalist party development. At the outset of his Administration the President gave an ear to the divergent views of a cabinet which included Jefferson as well as Hamilton and played a chairman-of-the board role, deliberating and deciding among alternative policy suggestions. As time passed, however, Washington himself and his Administration as a whole became more and more partisan; and by 1793 he was seeking advice almost entirely from a limited number of Federalist-minded leaders. Meanwhile, his portentous name was increasingly used as a distinctively Federalist symbol. Thus the Father of His Country became also the father figure of Federalist propaganda, a focus for partisan faiths, sentiments, and loyalties.

Reactions to new issues furthered the development of ideological ties. The French Revolution, at first widely hailed in America, ran its course toward regicide, radical republicanism, and (in February 1793) war with Great Britain. Determined to avoid involvement, Washington proclaimed a policy of official neutrality, a course Jefferson at the State Department accepted reluctantly in the face of treaties of commerce and alliance with France which had been signed in America's own hour of revolutionary trial. Yet to most Federalists the issue had become one of sanity against madness, stability against chaos, and their sentiments lay with the established order they thought England represented. The whole controversy prompted a war of words in which, as it intensified over the years, Federalist "Anglomen" came to stigmatize opponents with the cry of "Jacobin!" while opposition "Gallomen" responded with "Monocrat!" Though group or economic interests were not absent from the French-British issue in America, the controversy once again brought an emotionalized, philosophical, or symbolic cleavage of deeper faiths, convictions, and loyalties. In the ideological controversy the Federalists could perceive their party as a knightly band of saviors, the true champions of society, stability, and the nation. Irrational as attachment to Washington as father figure may have been, exaggerated as the logomachy over the French-British question was, these symbolic reactions and emotional ties completed the great transition from a Federalist faction to a Federalist party, as part of a general transition from old-style faction politics to modern party politics. They did so by reinforcing the seams of structure with crucial threads of emotional *élan*, of Federalist party spirit. . . .

Viewed in historical analysis and against the retrospect of American faction politics in the 1770's and 1780's, the emergence of the Federalists reveals a transition from the older "connexions" of fluid factions, family cliques, or juntos to the newer, modern connection of party. Four key distinctions between party on the one hand and faction on the other may be noted.

First, there is the matter of structure.

"Active leadership" and a "freely recruited following," as Max Weber has pointed out, "are necessary elements in the life of any party." Structure as the mark of party exists as a relatively durable or regularized relationship between leaders and followers. In America it has developed as a pattern of stable connections or relations between leaders at the center of government and lesser leaders, party workers or cadremen, and active participants at the outposts in states, counties, and towns. At the outposts, structure has extended to relations between local leaders, cadremen, or actives on the one hand, and the members of the public or electorate who support the party, and who constitute the party's following, on the other. By contrast, as early American experience reveals, factions lacked such stable relationships, consisting of *ad hoc* or shifting alignments as they generally did, limited to personal followings or capital coteries as they often were. Structure may or may not eventuate in full-scale organization, strictly construed as a regularized division of labor and co-ordination of activity toward a common set of goals. Nor does structure necessarily imply formal, mass membership in a party. American parties have been from the outset "cadre" parties in which active leaders and workers constitute the party as such, which in turn appeals to and mobilizes a freely attached following. The "mass" party of members ranged in local units was an invention of later times and other places, and has never been characteristic of American major party structure.

Next, parties contribute continuing procedures for performing certain key political functions. At a minimum, these functions include nominating candidates and campaigning in the electoral arena, and readiness to undertake management or the general conduct of public business in the governmental arena. In order to win elections or maintain power, however, and to win support for the policies they may espouse, parties also find it necessary in modern or mass politics to appeal to public opinion. In addition, if they are to succeed at management in government, they must establish some connection between decision-makers in various agencies of government—as, for example, the Federalist phalanx succeeded in doing between the executive branch and Congress. Finally, in order to maintain a power base, parties in a society with any significant measure of pluralism must find formulas of agreement that will bring disparate groups together, or play broker in gratifying, adjusting, or compromising conflicting interests. Thus parties move toward the performance of six critical functions: nominating; electioneering; shaping opinion; mediating among groups, "brokerage," or finding formulas of agreement; managing government; and supplying connections between the branches of government. Many of these functions were performed, though generally in hit-or-miss fashion, by early American cliques, factions, and juntos. In party politics as contrasted with faction politics, however, the functions are undertaken in a relatively more continuous, co-ordinated, and visible fashion, as they were by the Federalists. In party politics, furthermore, functions are typically interrelated in party action. The first purpose of party may be "to elect," to get its men into office; and American parties have usually shown more cohesion and greater activity in elections than in government management. Yet the very visibility and accountability of party in a free republic generates pressures for at least some success in government management, if the party is to succeed in later elections.

If a party embarks, as Hamilton and the Federalists did, on a course of innovative management, it must also turn to opinion formulation and electioneering to sustain that course.

In performing its functions, a party may develop a broad program, as a means of mobilizing group interests and public opinion and of strengthening its appeal in elections. This was the path Hamilton and the Federalists explored; and in years to come Madison, Jefferson, and the Republicans were to evolve a counter-program of their own. Indeed, the formulation of comprehensive statements of issues, positions, and policies has become almost a defining characteristic of modern parties. In pluralistic societies, such formulations must inevitably be designed to appeal to or accommodate the demands of various groups in the population. Thus they may often be somewhat contradictory in their terms, or more *pro forma* than meaningful in their substance. Yet, if only formally, they also represent a conception of public policy broader than the claims of particular groups, and in two-party systems they offer options for electoral choice not only on particular issues but on wide ranges of policy. When party programs are cogent for the times, reasonably coherent in their content, and meaningful, as was the Federalist program in the 1790's, they may serve as nationalizing forces, put some limits on the crosscurrents of localism and pluralism by polarizing opinion, and provide significant instruments for democratic functioning. In short, they may act as creative forces for coherence in the interplay of democratic politics.

To the two aspects of party as structure and functions, a third aspect may be added: range, density, and stability of support. Here is the idea of the interest-group foundations of parties stressed by such students of the American scene as Charles A. Beard, David B. Truman, and Wilfred E. Binkley. Generally parties, as contrasted with factions, encompass a wider range of groups in their power base; a greater density of the number of individuals enlisted in their followings as a ratio of all possible supporters; and a greater stability of alignments in the public. In a pluralistic democracy with a substantial electorate, party success inevitably entails a broad combination of groups, and a considerable ingathering of persons who identify with the party, not just in a given election or on a single issue, but over a period of years. Such, in Edmund Burke's language, are the links parties develop in a "just connexion with their constituents," in "public life (as) a situation of power and energy." By contrast, as the pre-party politics of the 1770's and 1780's reveals, cliques, juntos, and even substantial public factions generally are associated with a narrower range of group support, less dense followings, or greater fluidity of alignments in the electorate. A party combination may be built in Hamiltonian style, by joining parallel interests behind advocacy of a bold policy. More typically, it depends heavily on the brokerage function and on compromise to bind disparate interests and individuals into a working coalition. In any case, some measure of agreement, or what may be called concordance on outlook and policy, is an essential ingredient of ultimate party stability.

Finally, a party in the full sense entails a distinguishable set of perspectives; or ideology, with emotional overtones. As perspectives take on emotional or moral impact, beliefs develop into faiths, indentifications emerge as loyalties, ideas of right and wrong become moral commitments. If the men are available, attachments to revered leaders may reach charismatic intensity. As opposition appears, attitudes take on the cast of "in-group" as opposed to "out-group." Party outlooks are drawn in terms of "we" and "they"— our rightness and their wrongness, the goodness of having our leaders in office and the danger of having theirs, the "truth" of our doctrines and the "error" of theirs. The limited range of clique, faction, or junto politics rarely develops such broadly shared attitudes or highly emotional overtones. Certainly faction politics seldom generate the kind of emotional symbolism the Federalists attached to George Washington, or the broad ideological views they associated with European conflicts. Carried to extremes, the "we-they" perspectives of parties or ideological cleavages may disrupt a polity. Operating in moderation within a larger national agreement or emerging consensus, as they did on the American scene, they may advance party development or buttress party stability and cohesion. This can be so even in periods of party fatigue or comparatively empty politics-as-usual, when sentiments become increasingly vague, detached from immediately relevant issues, or flaccid. Even in such epochs, party loyalties and symbolism remain among the most tenacious of the ties that bind.

The concept of party sketched here—as structure, functions, substantial following, and in-group perspectives—is an analytical model. Thus stated in abstract form and related to the particular Federalist experience, the model may suggest a clearer consciousness in party building than America's political founders possessed, or greater order and clarity than the actualities of political hurly-burly ever reveal. This is the way of types or models, which are nevertheless useful as abstractions for purposes of inquiry. Parties are indeed instances of "an historical process," as V. O. Key has put it, and any model of their character must be elaborated as one traces their often disorderly development in different historical contexts. Nonetheless, the four criteria for party as contrasted with faction provide a basis for continuing analysis. . . .

The model underscores the ways in which party formations of the sort the Federalists generated are characteristically modern phenomena. Seen against the background of its time, the Federalist phalanx marked an important advance from the narrow, heavily personalized, tradition-bound, shifting "connexions" of eighteenth-century English or early American politics. The Federalist party was modern in that it was a relatively open, regularized political structure built around the free association of men from various walks of life, who evolved rationalized methods as efficient means to political goals and, in the era of emerging popular participation in politics, turned to propaganda and campaign tactics aimed at the mass of voters. It was modern also in the way in which its leaders and cadre workers devised orderly procedures to meet the claims of the plurality of interest groups thrown up by a developing economy, undertook to perform key political functions in a co-ordinated, regularized, consistent manner, and offered a generalized ideology and program. As the first formation of its kind, the Federalist party lacked the organization attained by parties in the Jacksonian era and in the twentieth century, and it never achieved the sweep of popular appeal which later parties were to enjoy. Organization, however, is not a necessary criterion of modern parties in the sense in which the term is used here, and the quality of popular response to parties varies even today. In one aspect after another, the Federalists in their time represented a distinctively new kind of political engine and realized in practice the major themes of political modernization.

The criteria of the model also enable us to say, not precisely when, but how faction politics ends as party politics begins. Thus the Federalist formation began as a capital faction, extended its lines into the states and communities, evolved a structure that proved durable, took on essential political functions, united a significant combination of interests, and developed an ideology and *élan*. We may speak of a Federalist party proper by the late months of 1793 and the early months of 1794—the period marked by Washington's adherence to Federalist advisers and attitudes, the ideological clash over foreign policy after the neutrality proclamation of April 1793, the final departure of Jefferson from the Cabinet, and a substantial consolidation of the Federalist voting alignment in Congress. Though a clique or faction here or there may exhibit one or more of the characteristics of party, it will not exhibit all of them together. When all four of the criteria "fit," a party is at hand.

The model also points to the crucial role of parties and a party system in a democratic polity. Faction politics tend to remain murky for the voter, prone to *ad hoc* combinations or majorities in decision-making which shift uncertainly from issue to issue, and thus ill-equipped to provide clarity of electoral choice or democratic accountability. While some of these characteristics may continue to lurk in multiparty politics, or in two-party politics characterized by loose multigroup formations or riven by intraparty factionalism, they are not likely to be so pronounced. Parties generally provide enlarged opportunities for popular participation and representation and for open and meaningful electoral choices, and thereby for democratic accountability. In a democracy, parties constitute the great stable links between public, electorate, and interest groups on the one hand, and governmental decision-making on the other. The utility of a party system for democratic functioning—even a loose, heterogeneous party system—can be seen most clearly if it is compared with the ways of faction politics. . . .

In an open, two-party system, one other thing is needed: the existence of and acceptance of an opposition. In America's great decade of political genesis, opposition to imperious Hamilton and his Federalist phalanx was forthcoming.

Signs of antipathy appeared with Hamilton's fiscal and bank proposals. As early as February 1791, Jefferson noted regretfully the existence of a strong "sect," oriented toward "monarchy." The answer, "the only corrective of what is corrupt in our present (trend) of government," was "the augmentation of the numbers of the lower house, so as to get a more agricultural representation, which may put that interest above that of the stock-jobbers." Sixteen months later, in June 1792, Jefferson complained again that the "sect" espoused the Constitution, "not as a good and sufficient thing in itself, but only as a step to an English constitution, the only thing good and sufficient in itself, in their eye." The answer once again was an enlargement, in the elections of 1792, of the national "representation" to counterbalance the capital "stock-jobbers and king-jobbers."

Such comments signalized an emerging resistance, a resistance led at first by other men who were far more vigorous in opposition than Jefferson himself was yet inclined to be.

Students of the American past often forget that historical developments in the United States were not unique, isolated phenomena but were related to long-term social changes occuring in the Western world. Modern political parties may have appeared first in the United States, but they eventually occurred elsewhere. The Americans created a republic at a time when monarchy was the norm, but the French soon imitated the American example and forces unleashed by revolution in France spread abroad. ROBERT R. PALMER (1909-   ), dean of the faculty at Princeton University, a specialist in French Revolutionary studies, is the author of a two-volume modern classic, *The Age of the Democratic Revolution,* which explores the breakup of old regimes on both sides of the Atlantic between 1760-1800, comparing the way different social orders faced the challenge of democratization. In the following selection, Palmer assesses the impact of the French Revolution on American politics.°

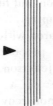

The French Revolution in American Politics

It was the Americans who had first given the example of rebellion, proclaimed the rights of man and the sovereignity of the people, and established a new public authority in their state constitutions by recognizing a constituent power in bodies called conventions. They had attracted the lively notice and admiration of dissatisfied persons in many parts of Europe. A mere fifteen years later the American image had already faded in a more blinding light on the screen of the world's opinion, and the mild accents of the heralds of liberty had been succeeded by a more ringing and compelling voice. If an influence had passed from America

to Europe before 1789, after that year the direction was reversed. If, as Barruel said, the "sect" had first shown itself in America, within two decades the United States was in the worthy position of a kind of Israel, and the ecumenical church, as embodied in the New Republican Order, had its center—complete with power, doctrines, and abuses—in Paris.

Like other countries, the United States felt the strong impact of the French Revolution. As elsewhere, the development was twofold. On the one hand, there was an acceleration of indigenous movements. On the other, there was an influence that was unquestionably foreign.

°Reprinted from *The Age of the Democratic Revolution: The Response* by Robert R. Palmer by permission of Princeton University Press. Copyright © 1964 by Princeton University Press. Pages 509-541. Footnotes omitted.

32

The latter presented itself especially with the war that began in Europe in 1792, and with the clash of armed ideologies that the war brought with it. The warring powers in Europe, which for Americans meant the governments of France and Great Britain, attempted to make use of the United States for their own advantage. Different groups of Americans, for their own domestic purposes, were likewise eager to exploit the power and prestige of either England or France. Some Americans saw the future of the United States best secured by a victory of the French Republic; others saw no hope for their own country except in a triumph by Great Britain. Political thought was also sharpened, heated emotionally, and broadened to the all-embracing dimensions that the word "ideology" suggests. American democracy, as expressed in the new Republican party, was shaped in part by the revolution in Europe; and American conservatism, as it came to be expressed by High Federalists, shared in some of the ideas of the European counter-revolution, especially as transmitted in books imported from England. The indigenous and the foreign became indistinguishable. In the way in which internal dissension passed into favoritism for foreign powers, the United States did not differ from the countries described from Ireland to Poland and from Scotland to Naples. . . .

It is widely agreed that the two American parties, and hence the beginnings of a two-party system, were produced in the United States by reactions to the European war and the French Revolution. The paradox, therefore, is that the ideological differences aroused in the United States, which became very heated, and the actual dangers of subservience to foreign powers, which were very real, may have contributed, by creating national parties to debate national issues and elect candidates to national office in an atmosphere of public involvement, to the solidarity of the union, the maintenance of the constitution, and the survival of the republic.

There was, to be sure, something peculiar in the entire phenomenon. Hamilton, who loathed the French Revolution, was more of a revolutionary than Jefferson both in temperament and in the policies that he espoused. He was more impatient of the compromises on which the federal constitution rested, he wanted to make over the country, and he would have liked, if he could, to abolish the states (especially Virginia) and replace them with small *départements* created by a national government, as in the French and other revolutionary republics in Europe. Jefferson, who sympathized with the French Revolution, was actually a good deal of a moderate, both in personality and in his ideas of what should be done. He spoke for a kind of liberty and equality that had long existed in America, and did not have to be fought for as in Europe, a liberty that meant freedom from government, and an equality of the kind that obtained among yeoman farmers—a way of life that had been threatened by British policy before 1775, and was threatened by Hamiltonian policy after 1790, in each case with the support of American "aristocrats" or persons aspiring to become such. Because of their different views on the need of change, it was Hamilton who was the "unitarist," and Jefferson the "federalist," in the sense then current in Europe, where, as has been seen, the radical democrats were unitarists, and the moderates inclined to the decentralization of power. The unitarist and "revolutionary" Hamilton was certainly no Jacobin, but he was the nearest that the

United States ever produced to a Bonaparte.

On a more general plane, also, the kinds of people who in the United States favored the French Revolution were not the same as in Europe. Nor were conservatives in America socially akin to those of Europe. There was a curious reversal or transposition. In Europe, on the whole, those who favored the French Revolution were middle-class people living in towns, including a good many bankers and businessmen, especially those interested in the newer forms of economic enterprise and development. Among the rural population, on the Continent, it was the landowners and property-owning farmers living nearest to the cities, most involved in a market economy, and enjoying the best communications with the outside world, who were most receptive to the Revolutionary ideas. In America the opposite was more nearly true. The business and mercantile community, and the farmers who lived nearest to the towns, or along the rivers and arteries of traffic and communication, were generally Federalist, and they became anti-French and anti-Republican. The same inversion holds for the counter-revolution, which in Europe was essentially agrarian. It drew its strength from the landed aristocracy, and from peasants who were politically apathetic, or looked upon cities as the abodes of their enemies. In the United States the Virginia gentry, and the farmers farthest from towns, along the frontier from Vermont through western Pennsylvania into Kentucky, were strongly Jeffersonian, Republican, anti-British, and partisan to the French Revolution. To this broad generalization various exceptions must be recognized, since in America (as in Europe) many urban "mechanics" and many of the professional classes, notably doctors, favored

the newly forming republicanism; but the cities in America were still small compared with those of Europe in any case; and the broad features of the transposition would appear to be valid.

This reversal of roles can best be explained by the differences between the United States and Europe, differences which Louis Hartz has summed up as the lack of the "feudal factor" in America. It was due also to a certain failure on the part of Americans, because of these very differences, to understand the Revolution beyond the Atlantic. In Europe the revolutionary movement, though it carried aristocratic liberalism and Babouvist communism at its fringes, was most especially a middle-class or "bourgeois" affair, aimed at the reconstruction of an old order, and at the overthrow of aristocracies, nobilities, patriciates, and other privileged classes. It is hard to see how Jefferson, who so much disliked cities with their moneyed men and their mobs, could have been so sympathetic to the French Revolution had he seen it in an altogether realistic light. The same is true of American democrats generally. But Hamilton and the Federalists were if anything even more mistaken. They imagined that men like themselves, in Europe, were as hostile to the Revolution as they were. Or rather, in their own self-definition, they failed to identify with the European urban middle classes, which they really resembled, and preferred to associate themselves with the British and European aristocracies, which they hardly resembled at all. Hamilton was a self-made man, a parvenu; even George Cabot, who became a very "high" Federalist, and whose family later became prominent, was the author of his own fortune, largely made in privateering during the War of Independence. These men could not see, and probably did not even know, that many men of business in Europe—the Watts and Boultons, Walker and Wilkinson, Gogel, Sieveking and the Bohemian banker, J. F. Opiz, were willing enough to sympathize with the ideas of the French Revolution in principle. . . .

The point is, of course, that both parties in America, far from being interested in an exact understanding of events, were using the current ideological arguments for their own purposes. Nor, for all the reversal of roles, were those arguments irrelevant to American issues. The bankers, merchants and shipping magnates who supported the Federalist party would not have been considered really high-class in Europe. In the class structure of America, however, they were upper crust; and the fact that there was no higher or older aristocracy for them to rebel against is what made it possible for them to be so conservative. The High Federalists seem to have thought (John Adams and merely moderate Federalists were not so sure) that the upper classes of the United States and Great Britain had a great deal in common. Aspiring to be aristocrats, they made themselves into legitimate targets for democrats. Appropriating the language of the European counter-revolution, they naturally found "republicans" arrayed against them. The great dispute in America was no mere comedy of errors, nor incongruous shadow-boxing; it was, as in Europe, a contest between different views on right and justice, on the form of the good society, and on the direction in which the world in general, and the new United States in particular, ought to move. . . .

To the constitution itself there was no basic opposition. Those who had argued against it in 1787, while the argument was open, accepted it in good faith after its ratification, and after adoption of the first

ten amendments to protect individual and state rights. Here again the difference from France and its sister-republics was pronounced. The divisions that formed in the 1790's did not prolong earlier differences over the constitution itself. That the anti-Federalists were unfriendly to the new constitution was an empty accusation; the chief founder of the Republican party, James Madison, was himself one of the authors of the new federal document, and co-author with Hamilton of the *Federalist* papers. If Madison and Jefferson, in 1798, toyed with ideas of "nullification," it was Hamilton and the High Federalists who, under pressure, were tempted by the thought of scrapping the constitution altogether. As the constitution itself was not a party issue, neither was "democracy" in the mere sense of the extent of the suffrage. The issue, as it developed, was the activation of voters whose right to the suffrage was not in question. As the decade passed, more men already qualified to vote actually voted.

At first, in 1790 and 1791, there was only Hamilton's program, and the opposition to it. Or rather, there were Hamilton's various measures, and sporadic critiques in which different individuals, in the new Congress and outside it, objected to some of these measures while accepting others. Hamilton, supported by Washington, took the view that the opposition was opposition to government itself. Since no parties of modern kind yet existed, nor was the idea or need of them even recognized, the issues soon took on larger dimensions, becoming a question of the propriety of opposition itself, or the right of citizens to disagree with, criticize, and work against public officials. In addition, Hamilton's plans required good relations with England. It may be that at this time, in the aftermath of the American Revolution, a dislike of England, or

rather of its government and social institutions, was a more positive and more
popular sentiment in America than was
affection for France. With France the alliance of 1778 was still in effect, and there
were memories of French aid in the late
war with England; but what aroused
fellow-feeling in America was the French
Revolution, since the French declaration
of rights, the new constitution, and the
vocabulary of debate, vindicating liberty
against tyrants, and equality against privilege, echoed what had been heard in
America for some time. When Adams and
Hamilton spoke out against the French
Revolution, they aroused others all the
more fiercely to its defense. A feeling
spread that the French Revolution was a
continuation of the American, and that
the American Revolution itself was en-
dangered, or unfinished.

In America, as in England and Europe,
the year 1792 was a turning point. The
war was seen by some as an outburst of
militant and destructive revolutionary
crusading, and by others, probably far
more numerous, as a defense against a
brutal intervention in French affairs by a
league of aristocrats and despots. The
proclamation of the French Republic was
seen by some as a piece of madness and
violence, and by others, far more numerous, as the dawn in Europe of a light
first seen in America. The French vic-
tories at Valmy and Jemappes were enthusiastically hailed. On February 1,
1793, the French declared war against
England; they were now fighting that old
bugbear of Americans, King George III.
News of this development came almost
simultaneously with the arrival of the first
minister of the French Republic, Edmond
Genet, who disembarked at Charleston,
South Carolina, on April 8, 1793. . . .

During the months of Genet's ministry
new political clubs began to form, the
democratic or republican societies. While
active Federalists had met in each other's
living rooms, or the public rooms of the
better hotels, people of a plainer sort now
began to meet in more modest quarters,
in taverns or country stores. Over forty
such clubs are known to have existed,
beginning in March 1793, chiefly in the
seaboard towns and along the frontier.
According to Oliver Wolcott they were
composed of "the lowest order of
mechanics, laborers and draymen"; and
Timothy Dwight, perhaps recalling a
famous remark of Burke's, thought that
democracy, like the devil, was entering
into "a herd of swine." It is true that the
societies had numerous members of in-
ferior station, but about half the membership was middle-class, consisting of
merchants, lawyers, larger landowners,
and a good many doctors. They somewhat
resembled the Sons of Liberty of the
1760's, or the radical clubs that sprang up
in England and Scotland in 1792, or similar groups in Holland, or the provincial
Jacobin clubs of France. They hardly resembled the Paris Jacobin club, which,
especially in 1793, was full of men active
in the government. Men in the American
government of republican opinions, such
as Madison and Jefferson, did not belong
to these clubs, which were of local, spon-
taneous, and popular origin. They were
not yet a political party but only a step in
that direction; most of them disappeared
within two or three years, as a more organized Republican party came into
being. Some of the clubs did take part
locally in elections, and it was these clubs,
apparently, that inspired the older
Tammany societies with political interests. Their attitude was one of suspicion of government and of officeholders, an anti-élitism, a class consciousness of a general sort pitting the
"many" against the "few". The tone was

suggested by the Ulster Democratic Club in the Catskills of New York which stood "on guard against designing men in office and affluent circumstances, who are forever combining against the rights of all but themselves." The clubs were opposed to Hamilton's policies, to British influence, and to fine gentlemen who used hair-powder or wore silk stockings. At a time when the newspapers carried more foreign than local news, they were fascinated by the great spectacle of the war in Europe. They were unanimously and excitedly pro-French. On the success of the French Revolution against its armed enemies, according to the prospectus of the Massachusetts Constitutional Society, in January 1794, depended the happiness of "the *whole world of Mankind.*"

To men who still conceived themselves as the proper guardians of society, suited by wisdom, experience, and position to form a governing class—that is, to most of the more articulate Federalists—this sprouting up of popular clubs, whose stock in trade was the criticism of government, seemed novel and alarming, if not revolutionary. When the farmers of Western Pennsylvania demonstrated against the new federal tax on spirits (in the so-called Whiskey Rebellion of 1794), it was charged that the clubs promoted insurrection, which was not true; but it was true that both the formation of clubs and the resistance to taxes expressed an antipathy to Hamilton's program, and indeed to government itself. President Washington called the clubs "self-created." He meant that they were extra-legal, and that only duly constituted bodies and duly elected representatives should deliberate or exert pressure on public issues; the phrase recalled what the British authorities had said of American correspondence committees twenty years before, and were saying of the London

Corresponding Society at precisely this moment. So far as the Federalists found themselves denying the legitimacy of any opposition to government arising outside government circles, the emerging Republicans could rightly accuse them of betraying the American Revolution. . . .

The American popular democrats, though not Jefferson and the Republican leaders might if left to themselves have welcomed, or even forced, another war with England (as in 1812), especially in view of the uncompromising demands of the British, which at times filled even Hamilton with dismay. John Jay went to England to negotiate a treaty. At the same time James Monroe went as minister to Paris, to maintain good relations with France while Jay tried to deal with England. Monroe, an enthusiastic republican, arriving just after the death of Robespierre, was very partial to the French Convention and to the Directory after it. Well disposed to democrats everywhere, he befriended Thomas Paine and Wolfe Tone in Paris. He was so eager to please the French that he sometimes failed to put the policies of his own government in their proper light. He believed that Jay in London was betraying him; he was so opposed to an American rapprochement with England that the French thought he must be deceiving them; and he seems not to have known, or to have been unconcerned, about French designs on the region west of the Alleghenies. Washington finally recalled him, and the ensuing uproar formed another stage in the differentiation of Federalists and Republicans. Meanwhile Jay negotiated his famous treaty, with Alexander Hamilton secretly working, through the British minister in Philadelphia, to satisfy the British in a way that even Jay thought too extreme. The British conceded practically nothing except evacuation of the

Northwest Territory. They refused to moderate their position on the impressment of sailors, or on matters of contraband, search, and seizure at sea in wartime; they refused to pay for American slaves taken off during the War of Independence (a sensitive matter to southern Republicans); and they refused to open their West Indian islands in a useful way to American commerce. The best that could be said in America for the treaty was that it prevented war with England. Undoubtedly such a war at this time would have been ruinous to the new republic, both from the impact of British power, and the effects of internal dispute and break-up within the United States. Politically, however, the argument was not a strong one; it sounded too much like appeasement.

It was in the controversy over the Jay treaty that the democratic movement grew into a Republican party, and that the Federalists closed ranks to obtain the goodwill of Britain, which was necessary both to their practical program and to their view of life and society. When Washington and the Senate ratified the treaty, debate raged in the House on measures for putting it into effect. The treaty became a question between government and opposition, or Federalists and Republicans. It raised also, above the prosaic problems of debt and taxation, and above localized grievances such as the excise on spirits, a question on which people of all kinds, throughtout the country, could form an opinion and become emotionally aroused. The question was seen, and strongly felt, as a choice between England and France, between two sides in an ideological war, between the old forces and the new in a contest without geographical boundaries, between monarchy and republicanism, Anglomen and Gallomen, men of sub-

stance and Jacobins—and between those who wished to move forward with a continuing American Revolution, and those who wished to restrain or qualify the implications of that event. On this basis the treaty was attacked and defended in the newspapers. Political leaders had an issue on which they could ignite public opinion, form connections with interested local groups, bring out the vote, and offer candidates for election on a basis of continuing principle, not merely of momentary issues or personal or passing factional groupings. The decisive bill to implement the treaty passed the House in April 1796 by a narrow margin, 51 to 48, on a clear party division. The two parties, Federalist and Republican, then girded for the presidential election of that year, which, with the retirement of Washington, was the first contested presidential election.

Both contenders for the office of President of the United States, in 1796, were denounced as the tools of foreign ideologies and foreign powers. Both parties presented themselves, their candidates, their opponents, and the issues in terms of the struggle raging in Europe. For Federalists, Jefferson was a Jacobin, an atheist, a libertine, a leveller, and almost a Frenchman. Adams was the friend of order, talent, and rational liberty. For the Republicans, Adams was a monocrat and an aristocrat who longed to mix with English lords and ladies; and Jefferson the upholder of republican principles. An electoral circular put out by the Republican Committee of Pennsylvania explained the choice. It was "between the uniform advocate of equal rights among citizens, or the champion of rank, titles and hereditary distinctions; . . . the steady supporter of our present republican constitution; or the warm panegyrist of the British Monarchical form of Government." That the bland Virginian was a Jacobin, or the irritable Boston lawyer an Anglomaniac, were about equally fantastic; but such was the atmosphere of debate. . . .

Adams was elected, but only by 71 electoral votes to Jefferson's 68. Jefferson became vice-president, but the Federalists remained in power, especially since Adams retained Washington's cabinet, which was composed of a group of strong Hamiltonians. In January 1797 the Paris *Moniteur* somehow obtained and published a copy of Jefferson's "Mazzei letter," written some months before at the height of the agitation over the Jay treaty. It caused an uproar on becoming known in America, but it was of course read in Paris also. The Frenchman could read, in his paper for 6 Pluviôse of the Year V, on the authority of the new American vice-president, that, though the American people remained soundly republican, the government was controlled by *un parti anglican-monarchico-aristocratique*. The editor remarked that the French Directory, by breaking relations with a government so perversely submissive to the English, would serve the cause of republicanism in the United States. It was now possible for the French, in their relations with the United States (as later for Americans in their relations to other countries) to feel that they could be hostile to its government while remaining friendly to its people.

In the following months, having imposed peace on Austria, the French hoped to do the same with England, and went to work on their plans for invasion. American Republicans, including Jefferson and the still unknown Andrew Jackson, looked forward with satisfaction to a French landing in England. "Nothing," wrote Jefferson, "can establish firmly the republican principles of our government but an establishment of them in England.

France will be the apostle for this." For other Americans such an event would signify the collapse of civilization. . . .

The clergy included, until 1795 or later, a good many who spoke sympathetically of the French Revolution from the pulpit. It was usual to attribute the signs of irreligion in France to the impostures of Roman Catholicism, and the violence of the Terror to the horrors of the Old Regime and the arrogance of European aristocrats. As Chandler Robbins said at Plymouth, quoting Solomon, oppression makes men mad. In the fall of the old system in France, Samuel Stillman saw "the judgment of God." Even the president of Yale, Ezra Stiles, hailed the execution of Louis XVI as a sign that European monarchs would soon be "tamed." The clergyman and geographer, Jedidiah Morse, as late as 1795, declared that the "irregularities" in France, including the atheism, were temporary and should be excused.

A change came about in 1795. For the clergy, and those who followed their lead, the publication of Paine's widely read *Age of Reason,* and the development of Elihu Palmer into a deistic lecturer who reached popular audiences, caused great consternation. It was realized that Christianity itself and not merely Roman Catholicism was being called into question. The French invasion of Holland and Switzerland, two Protestant countries highly regarded in America, made an unfavorable impression. In addition, by 1795 and 1796, party lines were being sharply drawn over the Jay treaty. Federalists became more committed to England than ever, and one way to expose and refute Republicans in America was to circulate increasing numbers of English books. . . .

Meanwhile Jedidiah Morse had stirred up a furor of his own. As late as 1795 he had sympathized with the French Revolution, but he learned from his correspondents in Edinburgh, in 1797, that Professor Robison was preparing a book showing the real causes of that upheaval, and he managed to obtain a pre-publication copy of Robison's work in Philadelphia. In 1798, just at the height of the XYZ excitement, Morse delivered two "fast day" sermons. He solemnly announced that the world was in the grip of a secret revolutionary conspiracy, engineered by the Order of the Illuminati—that Genet's clubs of five years before had been surface manifestations of this underground plot, and that the Republicans in America, recently so much in evidence, were the dupes or accomplices of this same pernicious organization, which labored everywhere, at all times, patiently, implacably, and behind the scenes, to overthrow all government and all religion. The publication of Robison's and Barruel's books served to confirm these allegations. An enormous outcry arose in the press. The Republicans were indignant. There were many skeptics, even among the New England clergy. For the Federalists such disclosures were welcome if not altogether believable; some odor of disreputability might be expected to cling

to the democrats; and in any case, following the usual psychology of such affairs, to wish to doubt or examine the charges might in itself be grounds for suspicion. On the whole, the scare soon blew over. The hostilities that it reflected were more lasting and more real.

Such was the state of the country during the presidency of John Adams—divided by interminable contention, bewildered by accusation and counter-accusation, flooded by propaganda, with its citizens appealing to foreigners in their disputes with each other, beset by laws against sedition and by their partisan enforcement, threatened by counter-resolutions putting the states above the federal government, carrying on actual hostilities with France at sea, and with important men clamoring for all-out war against that infidel republic, for which armies were being raised, American citizens prosecuted as if they were traitors, and alliance solicited with Great Britain.

As John Adams expressed it to Abigail, it was the corruption of Poland, with the roles of Russia and Prussia played by John Bull and Louis Baboon. He was captivated by neither.

Though William N. Chambers in a preceding selection challenges Charles Beard's contention that parties in the 1790s had roots in continuing rivalries among classes, he does not question Beard's account of the social sources of party development. In the following selection, PAUL GOODMAN (1934-   ), the University of California, Davis, examines in detail the make-up of the Jeffersonian Republican party in Massachusetts, one of the most populous and important states in the early Republic. Goodman contends that the Massachusetts evidence does not support a class interpretation such as Beard formulated. He argues that a multicausal explanation which recognizes that occupational groups are complex and often internally divided and that party preference is a function of social, religious, geographical, and other variables as well as economic interest makes more sense of the data than does Beard's thesis.°

Social Tensions and Party Development in Massachusetts

Party growth was painfully slow. The emergence of two rival groups at the national capital did not suddenly divide the rest of the country. Gradually, competitive parties evolved and by 1800 were spreading across the Commonwealth, penetrating sparsely settled areas in Maine,[1] bustling commercial towns along the coast, and quiet rural hamlets in the interior. The Democratic-Republican formation was a heterogeneous coalition of interests which cut across regional, economic, occupational, and religious lines. The party attracted persons alienated from established authority, convinced that those long entrenched in positions of influence blocked the advancement of worthy and ambitious though less favored citizens.

The party builders were not primarily national statesmen directing affairs from Philadelphia or professional politicians operating from Boston. Unlike later professional party leaders, they were generally ambitious merchants, tradesmen, capitalists, speculators, ministers, and office seekers who formed an interest and mobilized relatives, friends, acquaintances, and dependents to oppose those in

[1] Maine was part of Massachusetts until 1820.—Ed.

°Reprinted by permission of the publishers from Paul Goodman, *The Democratic-Republicans of Massachusetts, Politics in a Young Republic*, Cambridge, Mass.: Harvard University Press, Copyright, 1965, by the President and Fellows of Harvard College. Pages 70-127. Footnotes omitted.

power. As they fought for influence, they tried to swell the party showing at the polls by mustering wide support in the community. By linking together a varied collection of leaders and championing a broad spectrum of dissatisfied elements, the Republican party in Massachusetts formed a powerful alliance whose importance steadily mounted after 1800.

The common bond that united Republican Berkshire farmers with Salem merchants and rural Calvinists with urban rationalists was an interpretation of postrevolutionary experience. More than any other event, the French Revolution defined the content and style of politics. More than any other act, the Jay Treaty influenced the development of party. A strange and unreal debate developed in the 1790's which pictured two hostile groups, each dedicated to undermining the established order. Both linked their vision of the future and their understanding of the present with events abroad.

The general sympathy for France did not last much past 1793. As the Revolution turned radical and as war in Europe clouded the prospects of American neutrality, disillusionment spread. But many Americans did not lose faith. Those who became Republicans identified the cause of France with the cause of popular government everywhere. Britain's assault on Franco-American trade and her attempts to suppress enlightenment in Europe roused latent but highly nationalistic, anti-English emotions. If the French were defeated, Republicans believed, England would tyrannize the oceans and undermine American independence. The Jay Treaty confirmed fears that some groups at home, hostile to republican institutions, were anxious to tie the United States to the Tory kingdom. The treaty was "pregnant with Evil," Governor

Adams said, not simply because it sacrificed commercial interests, but because "it may restore to Great Britain such an influence over the Government and People of this Country, as may not be consistent with the general welfare." To Republicans the treaty meant abandoning neutrality, jeopardizing friendly relations with France, and becoming utterly dependent on Britain. Rejecting economic imperatives which drove many to accept the treaty, Republicans depicted their opponents as aristocrats bent on subverting the Republic. To defend the cause of republicanism at home and abroad, citizens formed societies in Boston, Portland, and throughout the nation.

The appearance of these organizations aroused deep suspicion because they resembled the feared Jacobin clubs of France, which had seized control and engulfed the nation in a blood bath. The Republican societies might be the vanguard of a movement to subvert established authority and remake America in the image of France, where the mob ruled and distinctions of rank and wealth vanished.

A harsh and divisive dialogue pervaded the political atmosphere. Men argued not over means but over ultimate ends. Republicans pictured their antagonists as aristocrats, British agents, former Tories, and refugees; Federalists characterized their adversaries as levelers, Jacobins, and anarchists dedicated to upsetting the settlement of 1789. Each condemned the other for placing enthusiasm for a foreign power over loyalty to the Union. Both images were unreal, bearing but a faint connection with the inclinations of either group. Yet they rested on a semblance of truth, because extremists on both sides lent substance at times to the parties' images of the other.

More   important,   however,   the

dominant elements in both parties were loyal to the arrangement of 1789. Republicans praised the French Revolution but would never accept political theory or practice that violated traditional notions of constitutionalism. Jeffersonians did not relish the violence of revolutionary change abroad and had no plans to alter the distribution of wealth or to remodel the social structure at home. Most Federalists were similarly devoted to preserving the settled order. They became hostile to the Revolution because they believed the French had rejected the politics of balance and overturned established authority without stabilizing a new one. Except for some highly placed extremists, however, few Federalists had serious intentions of recasting America in the image of Britain. The party had its share of old patriots who regarded England primarily as the major bulwark against the spread of Gallic influence and the key to the nation's economic health.

Paradoxically, while both parties were committed to the existing polity, disagreement appeared more fundamental, the political dialogue more intemperate, and the possibilities of compromise seemingly fewer than in almost any other period of American history. The roots of this conflict are to be found in the unstable and dynamic character of post-revolutionary American society.

Eighteenth century Massachusetts was neither a pure democracy where the people ruled directly nor a closed preserve dominated by a hereditary elite. From the earliest days, political power dispersed and fell into the hands of clusters of local groups. Ambitious and rising newcomers were able to gain access to office and enter the local gentry, becoming the judges, justices of the peace, tax assessors, sheriffs, ministers, lawyers, doctors, and traders who constituted the ruling elite. Though farmers and artisans were usually content to let men of substance guide the community, many could vote, demand justice, turn out an old representative, and attach themselves to factions eager to challenge long-entrenched interests. But generally officials expected and enjoyed popular acquiescence.

The Revolution did not tear apart the social fabric. In many towns the county leaders were patriots, and little displacement occurred, while in other communities Tories fled or retired from public life and old-line families made way for the new. The war opened numerous opportunities for men in the lower ranks of the gentry to gain prominence and improve their positions through military service, politics, and trade. Thus continuity and change were both part of the revolutionary experience. While the war did not cause the wholesale displacement of one group by another, it did alter the social structure, creating opportunities for many who lacked the wealth, family, or experience that characterized the older elites. As untrained and inexperienced men appeared on the scene competing for recognition, it was no longer as clear as it once had been who was entitled to lead. Moreover, even as the governing groups settled down and became better defined, they faced unprecedented problems: wartime economic dislocation, constitutional changes, and the formation of a viable union in place of the Confederation.

Two great crises followed the Revolution—Shays' Rebellion and the debate over ratification. Twice citizens challenged traditional leadership, but the threats to the social order proved brief and not entirely successful. By 1790 Massachusetts and the nation had moved fast and far toward mastering discontent and pacifying the unruly. Confronting armed hostility, the judges and militia leaders, doctors and lawyers, merchants and capitalists, newcomers and oldtimers, stood united against disorder. The conflict over the Constitution, however, was less clearcut, though most of the gentry finally favored ratification.

But the unity of the 1780's did not last, because the social order was unstable. While the Revolution created new opportunities, it also weakened the traditional lines of authority. Groups who themselves had but recently arrived lacked the force of tradition and custom to buttress their position. Moreover social mobility—the openness of professions, the varied chances in trade, the creation of new communities requiring leadership, and the rise in older communities of newcomers aspiring to prominence—left persistent sources of tension. In this social context, two rival groups in the 1790's competed to guide the Commonwealth's future.

Men's positions in the social structure shaped their responses to the events of the decade. Those most securely established in local office, trade, and finance, those controlling the seats of authority in church and state, came to view the French Revolution with horror. Fearing that involvement would undermine prosperity, they also believed that the spread of French doctrine threatened the social order. They recoiled from Jacobinism, clung to the protection of a British alliance, and attempted to uproot subversion at home. Well-placed individuals such as the judges, justices, probate officers, county treasurers, sheriffs, the complex array of entrenched officials together with the older county families and their professional and mercantile allies, led the Federalist party.

The sources of Republican leadership were different. The party attracted persons either outside the elite or enjoying a recently acquired and insecure position in local society. They were often new men who came from rising families that had been excluded from the highest levels of influence and standing. Frequently men of substance in their own communities, they desired but lacked countywide influence, and unlike some of the newly arrived had not gained a firm position in the social order. Rising from obscurity or modest circumstances, they identified revolution and republicanism at home and abroad with opportunity. The French had uprooted privilege, destroyed ecclesiastical and monarchic establishments, and had given power to those who had been excluded for centuries. Americans who condemned change and feared and distrusted popular rule cast doubt on the validity of republicanism.

Federalism, according to Republicans, threatened the future of the newcomer, the ambitious man, the outsider. To a few, the Hamiltonian financial system spelled the creation of a monied aristocracy that would rule the land and widen the distinctions between various levels of society. Federalist partiality for Britain appeared to mark that corrupt kingdom as a model for American imitation. Federalist foreign policy moved the nation closer to war with France, bringing with it heavy taxes and the persecution of dissent. Federalist commercial policy doomed newly developed and profitable ties with France and the Continent. Within Massachusetts itself, Federalists hoarded power and privilege, narrowing rather than widening opportunity. The party stood for monopoly of local office, charter privileges, the natural resources of Maine, and the religious, institutional, and professional life of the community.

The nation was misruled, Republicans announced, because government did not truly reflect the interests of the people. Voters were often deceived and lacked direct representation. For generations they had submitted to a system of indirect rule whereby the lawyer, not the merchant, the local judge, not the farmer, sat in the General Court. But indirect government did not always work. It suffered anarchic breakdown in the 1780's and now a decade later once again was under heavy attack. Republicans repeatedly demanded direct representation. Communities should select men whose interests closely reflected those of the voters. Merchants, not lawyers, should sit for the trading towns; farmers, not judges, should represent the inland communities. Only then would an identity exist between voters and officials.

The Republican appeal was essentially an attack on traditional sources of leadership, not a call for social upheaval but a demand for enlarged opportunities for the excluded. Finding difficulty in meeting the argument, Federalists rehearsed the notion of a harmony of interest and denounced their critics as "ignorant rich men" eager for power. The Republican polemic proved to be more than shrewd propaganda: it worked. Merchants such as Orchard Cook and Jacob Crowninshield, farmers such as Joseph B. Varnum, and mechanics such as Thompson Skinner replaced many of the Federalist attorneys who sat in Congress. By questioning the assumption by which Federalists ruled, Republicans hoped to gain influence. The obstacles to opportunity must be weakened and above all the nation must avoid war with France and entanglement with Britain. The channels of trade with the Continent and the Far East must remain open; expansive measures must replace repressive political and economic ones; access to corporate privilege must become available to everyone; and the professional and communal life of the state must comprehend groups that had been excluded previously. These were the general objectives of the Republican interest; their precise formulation varied. Eastern merchants were concerned with foreign trade and sharing in grants of corporate charters, while their inland allies were moved by other problems. But everywhere Jeffersonians joined to remove the barriers to advancement.

After two decades of struggle, the party enjoyed considerable success. In many communities Republicans became the dominant group, replacing the older leadership or at least sharing influence. In time they merged into the social order and eventually distinctions blurred and became almost imperceptible. Party labels lost their meaning as the older differences narrowed and eventually disappeared, yet the experience of rivalry in the early Republic left a discernible trace. Amid the bitterness of political warfare, fine distinctions of position were maintained. Striving to achieve a coherent and secure place in New England life, Republicans constituted a social group united by ties of kinship and marriage. The Austins, Townsends, and Gerrys intermarried, as did the Harrises and Devenses of Charlestown; out in the Connecticut Valley marriage cemented ties between the families of William Lyman and Samuel Fowler. Eastern Republicans such as William Eustis and James Swan formed connections with the Langdons, New Hampshire's leading Jeffersonian family. The formation of Republican social connections was only one aspect of the processes by which aspiring elements united to further their interests. The party's development did not follow precisely the same course everywhere, but an examination of the sources of the Republican interest will indicate the character of the movement.

Throughout the rural communities of Massachusetts, from Middlesex to Hampshire County, from the eastern District of Maine to the western Berkshires, Republican groups challenged the reigning authorities. They did not enjoy equal success everywhere; in some areas outstanding leadership failed to compete with entrenched elements and circumstances were unfavorable to dissent. Out in the Berkshires, however, one of the earliest successful Republican organizations developed in the 1790's.

Berkshire County was settled later than all other parts of the Commonwealth except Maine. As a consequence, its social structure was looser. Many of the towns were recently founded, others were not yet incorporated at the time of the Revolution, and local centers of power were often ill-defined. Life seemed freer, less trammeled by settled ways and institutions than in the older parts of the state. Here religious dissent flourished and some of the purest heirs of Jonathan Edwards' Calvinism maintained the faith against the liberalism of the commercial east. Here men moved to start afresh, to found their churches, and to win for themselves and their families greater control over their destinies.

Despite its frontier qualities, Berkshire had a ruling gentry drawn from wealthy early settlers who carried family authority from the Connecticut Valley into the hills further west. The names most commonly identified with Berkshire leadership at the time of the Revolution included the Dwights, the Ashleys, the Williamses, and their brilliant professional ornament, Theodore Sedgwick. But officialdom here

was less secure, less well entrenched than elsewhere, and it was not surprising that the Revolution evoked demands from newcomers that power be shared. The northern towns had been growing more rapidly, demanded change, and provided leadership for the Berkshire constitutionalists in the late 1770's. The constitutionalists closed the courts and favored reforms broadening the base of participation in government. In the end they forced the Dwights and Williamses to compromise, and as a result county leaders were united when the Shaysites challenged authority. But after the suppression of the rebels, tensions persisted in the upper levels of society, and by 1794 an opposition to the Sedgwick connection had become active and powerful.

Several figures typified Berkshire Republicanism. Thompson J. Skinner, Jr., was the most influential Jeffersonian in the far west. A brigadier general of the militia, state senator and treasurer, twice elected to Congress, federal marshall, and commissioner of loans, he was the center of an important interest. He was the son of a Connecticut minister, became a mechanic, and migrated to Williamstown in 1775, where, with a brother, he was a carpenter and builder. Skinner emerged as one of the new leaders of the growing northern part of the county. He resisted the Shaysites and voted for the Constitution in the ratifying convention, but after 1790 he split with the old county leadership. . . . Skinner's position on the important public questions of the day was often unclear, for his campaigns reflected political shrewdness rather than a clearcut programmatic commitment. . . . The Skinner forces struck their most consistent note when they professed faith in popular government and attacked rule by "the high ton'd Aristocrats, Monocrats, Demagogues, Pedagogues, Gogmagogs, Conspirators, and Federal Hopgoblins," who were usually pettifogging lawyers anxious to destroy liberty.

Throughout the county men of talent and ambition joined Skinner.... A somewhat different brand of Berkshire Republicanism was represented by John Bacon and Reverend Thomas Allen, both Calvinists. Bacon graduated from Princeton in 1765 and preached at the Old South Church in Boston, where his Calvinism resulted in dismissal and retreat to a more hospitable environment. He opposed the constitutionalists and the Shaysites but changed his mind at least twice on the federal Constitution. A firm democrat, fearful of aristocratic designs, he was the only state senator to condemn the Alien and Sedition Laws. A consistent and outspoken critic of Hamiltonian finance, he was suspicious of banking and speculation, identifying lawyers and financial interests with antirepublicanism and deism. ...

Sharing Bacon's Calvinism and hostility to the entrenched judiciary were two of the most prominent religious figures in the Berkshires. Reverend Thomas Allen, the Congregationalist minister of Pittsfield, was born in Northampton, where the family supported Jonathan Edwards, and he grew up a New Light Calvinist. Educated at Harvard, he settled in Pittsfield in 1764, preaching there for forty-six years. A prominent constitutionalist and anti-Shaysite, Allen did not seek political office but became a conspicuous example of Jeffersonian Calvinism. Elder John Leland shared with Allen the religious leadership of Berkshire Republicanism. An outstanding itinerant Baptist preacher, he spent his early career in the South, later migrating north to reclaim his native New England from sin. Settling in the town of Cheshire amid a large group of Rhode Island Baptists, Leland shared

Allen's hostility to the judiciary, which stood between the people and government and enforced oppressive laws requiring men to support established churches.

During the 1790's Skinner, Bidwell, Allen, Leland, the Bacons, and others began building a Republican organization and bidding for political office. A series of vacancies in county offices enabled Governors Hancock and Adams to appoint Skinnerites. By 1800 Republicans held a majority of the important positions, including most of the places on the Court of Common Pleas and those of the probate judge and sheriff. Success increased the power and prestige of the leadership, and after 1800 Berkshire became a Jeffersonian stronghold. ...

Religious problems aroused men because they were local and personal, and because they stimulated disputation by many of the most articulate members of the community. The growing controversy over the establishment was important not only because of the substantive issues involved, but also because it gave parties a cause which cut across sectional, economic, and class lines. Advocacy of the separation of church and state gave Republicans a popular issue which appealed to large groups dissatisfied with the standing order and opened fresh possibilities of forging new links between the party and the people. ...

Jeffersonian Calvinists, all sorts of dissenters, and the Republican leadership found common interests in opposition to Federalist authority in church and state. Since clerical influence and secular power supported each other, an attack on one would weaken both. The Republican leadership thus sought to become the champion of dissent and disestablishment. Early in his first term, Jefferson issued an address to propagate the principles of separation. In Massachusetts, Levi Lincoln, William Eustis, and Charles Jarvis had long sympathized with those opposed to ministerial taxes. James Sullivan was the legal defender of the sects, which in Maine found a friend in William King. Jeffersonians repeatedly called on dissenters to "cement the basis of civil and religious Liberty, by confounding the artifices of those *Anglo*-federalists, who would establish an hierarchy in Massachusetts, and suppress the freedom of Divine worship."

Bay State Jeffersonians planned carefully. When they learned that Tom Paine intended to publish a third volume of the *Age of Reason*, they asked the ancient Sam Adams to induce Paine not to embarrass the party any further in New England. For Massachusetts Republicans hoped to nurture the growth of theistic faith. "It deserves a thought," the Reverend William Bentley wrote, "how much the common interest of mankind will be served by weakening the Congregational Churches, by strengthening the Baptists, by deposing the more enlightened sect & not putting any check to superstition." Bentley and his Republican congregation in Salem were moving toward Unitarianism and had no personal sympathy for "illiterate enthusiasts," but they contemplated religious variety "as favorable to religious liberty" and to the cause of the party. Consequently, they shrewdly gave financial support to local dissenters. "The Baptists have finished & dedicated their new Brick Meeting House," Bentley wrote. "They boast much of it & not one of them has yet discovered that the Republicans built it. It is not amiss they should think it their own." Thus eastern Republicans attempted to forge a link with popular religion. Viewing the establishment as a bulwark of Federalism, they hoped to undermine both by fostering multiplicity.

On this basis, Bay State Republicanism could unite rural Calvinists and urban rationalists, inland dissenters from the religious order and urban critics of the social order. It was through such processes that a diverse coalition of far-flung interests became a political party. Political change in the eastern maritime communities and the District of Maine further enlarged, broadened, and strengthened the Republican formation.

In urban communities up and down the Massachusetts coastline a strong Republican party challenged Federalism's right to speak for the maritime interest. Traders, capitalists, and mechanics whose welfare Federalist rule threatened forged a new political instrument seeking to reshape the young Republic. . . .

Urban interests had never been monolithic; fissures had always existed, for the varied and complex groups who populated the port towns had numerous and conflicting ideas of how best to advance their welfare. The prospect of war with France, however, heightened differences and polarized groups. Rising entrepreneurs, whose fortunes rested directly on commercial ties with France, together with others whose advancement required both peace and access to privilege long enjoyed by the well-established, challenged Federalist control of the maritime towns. . . .

The rise of eastern Republicanism revealed that urban groups had complex and differing views of self-interest. Allied with dissenters and Calvinists in the rural towns, together with newcomers who were challenging Federalist authority, Republicans also found powerful support in the District of Maine, where the emergence of a Jeffersonian connection mirrored the processes of party evolution throughout the Bay State.

Linked to Massachusetts until 1820, Maine was both New England's frontier and the fastest growing part of the Commonwealth. Extensive, unoccupied land, untapped natural resources, and numerous harbors invited men to settle afresh. Between 1790 and 1810 the population of the District of Maine advanced twice as fast as that of Massachusetts as a whole, and Maine's voters became a valuable prize for the party which captured them. Safely Federalist until 1800, Maine was rapidly transformed into a Republican bastion, indispensable to the party's success.

The pace and pervasiveness of social change defined the contours of Maine politics. Sparsely settled before the Revolution, the District boomed in the postwar years as pioneers poured into its virgin lands. Rapid settlement undermined the older social order, for newcomers challenged the established leadership. Within this dynamic context, politics was highly factious, parties emerged slowly and complexly, and most of the Republicans prominent after 1800 had taken little part in public life during the preceding decade. As the population doubled between 1790 and 1800, new men gained wealth and influence, some becoming leaders in the new communities, others competing for position in the older towns. Maine Republicanism thus represented the thrust of enterprising and ambitious elements struggling for recognition and power.

The party was extremely weak during the 1790's, most of its strength being concentrated among the farmers and lumbermen of the Kennebeck Valley, who rallied behind Henry Dearborn. A revolutionary veteran who settled in the valley after the war, Dearborn advanced rapidly, buying and selling land and running lumbering operations, as well as a wharf, store, and ferry. In 1790 he became federal marshall and two years later was elected congressman from the huge district comprising Lincoln, Hancock, and Washington counties. By supporting Madison in 1794 in opposition to Federalist foreign policy, he alienated influential groups back home. Dearborn lost his seat in 1796 and returned to his home to battle for local supremacy.

Both Lincoln and Kennebeck counties were dominated by old families, allied with some fortunate recent arrivals who enjoyed access to authority. The Lithgows of Hallowell and the Bowmans of Pownalborough had a firm grip on local office even before the Revolution. Members of their families held multiple offices and passed them on from one generation to the next. Together with the Norths, the Conys, the Dummers, and others they were the judges and justices, the sheriffs and leading attorneys, of the local elite. Though often divided by personal rivalries, the threat of Jacobinism welded them into a cohesive group anxious to preserve their power. Opposition to Federalist foreign policy isolated Henry Dearborn from these most prominent men in the Lincoln-Kennebeck country.

Republican influence grew, however, as able and ambitious individuals throughout the region enlisted in the cause. Some were fairly well established, such as Nathan Weston of Augusta. Weston had been a merchant, ran a general store, purchased furs and lumber, and manufactured pot and pearl ashes, regularly running a vessel to and from Boston. In the 1790's he contested Daniel Cony's leadership in Augusta, and though unsuccessful at first eventually was elected to the General Court and served on the Council. Another prominent Kennebeck Republican, John Chandler, was born in New Hampshire and served in the Revolution. His friend Dearborn induced him to remove with a party of neighbors to Monmouth, Maine. Poor and illiterate, Chandler went to school with the children, worked as a blacksmith, and dug potatoes for General Dearborn. With patronage, he rose fast, becoming a census taker, postmaster, ensign in the militia, and tavernkeeper. He later was a representative, a state senator, and a congressman. Together with Chandler, Weston, Barzillai Gannett, Francis Carr, Martin Kinsley, Eleazar Ripley, and other Republican hopefuls in Kennebeck and Penobscot country, Dearborn constructed an influential connection. Jefferson appointed him Secretary of War in 1802 and collector of the Port of Boston later.

The rise of the Dearborn group, however, only partially defines the sources of Maine Republicanism. Without the support of important mercantile elements along the coast, the party would have remained a minority. Two powerful groups of Republican merchants made York and Lincoln counties Jeffersonian strongholds. Although the party emerged late along the seabord, it grew on opposition to Federalist foreign policy, which many feared would lead to war with France.

The Cutts connection of Saco (Biddeford) was the center of the Republican interest in York County. The founder of the family fortune, Thomas Cutts, started as a clerk for Sir William Pepperell, borrowed £100 capital from his father, and entered business in Saco. Here he prospered and became the richest man in the community, owning many vessels, engaging in overseas trade, acquiring extensive landholdings, and assuming the attributes of the local gentry. He built a great mansion, educated his children, and was generous to the poor. Although the elder Cutts was justice of the peace and a notary public, he never achieved rank as a county official.

Until 1798 York was a one-party county, repeatedly sending Federalist George Thacher to Congress by overwhelming majorities. But toward the end of the decade opposition appeared in Saco. Like many traders elsewhere, the Cuttses had commercial ties with France and feared that war would disrupt profitable relations with the Continent. In the middle of the 1790's the family was trading with Hamburg, Amsterdam, and particularly Bordeaux, carrying freight to France for Josiah Bacon, a Republican merchant in Boston. In 1796 Cutts was trying to collect payment from the French firm of Dallarde, Swan & Co. Allied with other respectable men in York such as Stephen Thatcher and Joseph Storer, who were Kennebunk merchants, John Woodman, a prominent Buxton farmer and local worthy, Benjamin Green, a Berwick teacher and lawyer, and Dr. Thomas G. Thornton, physician and merchant in Saco, the Cuttses won control of York County and became one of the great Republican commercial forces in Maine. In 1802 they sent Thomas' Harvard-educated son Richard to Congress and for years the family dominated the county, resisting attacks by factious elements who considered them hightoned aristocrats.

Even more influential was the mercantile group led by William King of Bath. King was a great merchant-politician, powerful not merely in Lincoln County but throughout Maine and Massachusetts. From all over the state and from Washington, Jeffersonians sought his advice on policy, patronage, strategy, and tactics.

King was born in 1772, the son of a Scarborough merchant and brother of two other prominent public men, Rufus King, a Federalist senator and diplomat from New York, and Cyrus King, a Federalist lawyer in Saco. Unlike his two brothers, William did not go to college and had few advantages. He went to work in a Saco sawmill and later formed a partnership with Dr. Benjamin I. Porter, acquiring a mill at Topsham, a center of the lumber industry. Here Porter and King opened a store, purchased timber for export, and operated several vessels. Moving to Bath in 1800, King retained his connections with Porter and Topsham but was now more favorably situated to expand his activities. He opened a store with Peter H. Green, obtained wharves, warehouses, and additional shipping, and helped to establish Maine's first textile mill. . . .

As King prospered, he also entered local politics, representing first Topsham and then Bath in the General Court. In the 1790's he was a Federalist, thus belonging to the predominant party in the maritime communities of his region. But around 1800 Lincoln County split, paralleling divisions elsewhere in eastern Massachusetts. While the Dearborn Republicans of the upper valley of the Kennebeck and Penobscot ran their own candidate for Congress, the old-line Federalist leadership met resistance from a younger group led by King. For several years the two factions fought for power, at first within the party; by 1804 the King interest had moved into the Republican camp, had routed the Federalists, and had become the dominant power in Lincoln County.

The King forces charged their Federalist opponents with being violent Hamiltonians, enemies of President Adams, and supporters of war. They appealed to farmers and merchants to vote for Orchard Cook, a Wiscasset trader who would support the Republican administration because it was "the firm advocate for peace which is favorable to trade." Peace, they insisted, would advance the prices farmers received by 50 per cent, ensure merchants the advantages of neutral trade, and provide mechanics with employment in an expanding shipbuilding industry. Claiming the backing of the wealthiest shipowners in the district, the Cook people announced that merchants had "at length become sensible that their interest is to be promoted only by delegating some of their own profession to assist in legislating on their important commercial concerns." With more than forty lawyers in Congress, the time had come for Lincoln County to elect a Republican trader to join Cutts of York County and Crowninshield of Salem. The anti-Cook Federalists described their rivals as "ignorant rich men" who sought to prejudice "the people against men in power that they may be removed to make way for others of aspiring dispositions."

King's group won in 1804 and became extremely powerful in Maine politics. Jeffersonians appreciated the importance of this development and welcomed the new converts. "Gentlemen of talents & property," wrote Joseph Bartlett to King in 1805, "are ever an acquisition to any party." "Your district has effected an unexpected change," Congressman Richard Cutts had noted earlier, adding, "Mercantile Genl. are much wanted here."

The rise of the King connection illustrates the dynamic quality of party evolution in the early Republic. King and his circle were successful, newly risen traders dissatisfied with established leadership. Desiring access to power to obtain patronage, land, bank, and insurance charters and other perquisites of influence, they found difficulty advancing their interests as Federalists. Apprehensive that extreme Federalism threatened peace and prosperity, they sought to control the party and later deserted it for Republicanism. They also perceived that rising popular discontent within Maine offered fresh opportunities for ambitious, clever, and aggressive new-comers. By championing the cause of landless farmers and religious dissenters, Maine Republicans broadened their appeal and forged a powerful coalition which soon dominated the District.

Dissent grew and flourished in Maine more vigorously than anywhere else in the Commonwealth. Here, as elsewhere, the sects complained that they paid ministerial taxes to support the Congregational establishment. By advocating reform and attacking Federalism as the bulwark of the standing order, Jeffersonians captured much of the sectarian vote. In Maine, as in Massachusetts proper, Republicans and dissenters found a harmony of interests, each group advancing its own cause by uniting against Federalist authority.

Republicans also were spokesmen for another underprivileged group, the landless squatters. Burdened by a heavy postwar debt, Massachusetts used its public domain as a source of revenue. It granted some land to war veterans and might have offered yeomen small free farms, but instead it sold large tracts to realize immediate gains, notably by the Bingham Purchase, which transferred some two million acres to private interests. At the same time, the Commonwealth sought to promote settlement and improvement by requiring grantees to plant a given number of families on each township within a stipulated time. The program proved unsuccessful, for it raised relatively little money and failed to stimulate migration. The Bingham interest, for instance, was unable to meet its obligations and repeatedly won postponements, and settling duties were neither performed nor enforced. In addition to the postwar grants, numerous large ones made during the colonial period became a recurrent source of controversy because of disputes over their validity and precise boundaries. Control of extensive and disputed holdings by absentee proprietors was thus a potential cause of tension. . . .

The squatters argued that speculators had violated their contracts by defaulting on the settlement duties, and therefore had forfeited their titles. Moreover, farmers who had bought, expecting that development would be actively pushed, had been cruelly deceived. Husbandmen charged that the Pejepscot proprietors refused to sell on reasonable terms as directed by resolutions of the General Court. They argued that they had been forced to pay twice for their farms, and some owners were even accused of selling public lands. For years unrest festered. There were occasional acts of violence against surveyors, but not until after 1800 did the problem assume serious dimensions. When absentees began to bring suits of ejection, discontent mounted, violence flared, and law and order were flouted. The time was overripe for the state to formulate a just and equitable solution to Maine's land problems.

Republicans such as William King realized that the party might contribute to a peaceful settlement while gaining popularity. Proprietors played into their hands because their ties were usually Federalist, enabling Republicans to claim that they were the yeomen's only true friends. By 1805 and 1806 alarmed Federalists warned that the squatters of Maine would impose a Republican governor on the Commonwealth. Jeffersonians replied: "The squatters must come forward with their usual strength."

The squatters, dissenters, merchants, and office seekers of Maine who formed the Republican party were highly successful. In a few years they transformed the eastern counties from a Federalist bastion into a Republican stronghold, which gave the party 60 per cent of its vote. Rapid change and social instability along New England's eastern frontier fostered the growth of a strong Republican connection, but the pattern of party evolution in Maine only duplicated the pattern throughout the Commonwealth wherever ambitious and aggressive newcomers and climbers challenged the dominance of established authority. Successful merchants and rising local worthies, fearful of war with France and anxious for the preferments of power, joined with religious dissenters and landless squatters to reorder public life and broaden opportunities in the germinal years of the young Republic. . . .

As the Federalists' chief propagandist and strategist, Alexander Hamilton tirelessly and cogently defended his party's policies and defined its philosophy. In the following selection, CLINTON ROSSITER (1917-   ), analyzes Hamilton's ideas about man and society and illuminates the nature of the beliefs shared by many though not all Federalists. Hamilton's political philosophy helped to generate party conflict, which he deplored since he viewed the Federalists as the only legitimate promoters of the general welfare. Though Hamilton's philosophy helped him to gain national prominence and power, it also was responsible, in part, for his party's downfall. John L. Senior Professor of American Institutions at Cornell, Rossiter has written extensively on the American political tradition, sympathetically exploring the conservative position that usually regards Hamilton as one of its patron saints.°

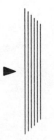

Alexander Hamilton and the Politics of Federalism

A man of action who roused to the challenges of assembly, courtroom, and field of battle, Hamilton was also a man of thought who found comfort and inspiration among the books in his study. In a letter to his friend James A. Bayard of Delaware, in whose hands chance had placed the power to decide the disputed election of 1800, he explained why, much as he hated Jefferson, he simply could not prefer Burr as President of the United States:

The truth is, that Burr is a man of very subtle imagination, and a mind of this make is rarely free from ingenious whimsies. Yet I admit that he has no fixed theory, and that his peculiar notions will easily give way to his interest. But is it a recommendation to have *no theory?* Can that man be a systematic or able statesman who has none? I believe not. *No general principles* will hardly work much better than erroneous ones.

This letter, one of the most fascinating from Hamilton's pen, is an admirable introduction to the political thought of an eminently "systematic" and "able" statesman. He had a strong preference for men of intellect in public life because he was himself a man of intellect, and because he did not see how he could have achieved even the first of his goals if he

°From *Alexander Hamilton and the Constitution*, © 1964, by Clinton Rossiter. Reprinted by permission of Harcourt, Brace & World, Inc. Pages 113-149. Footnotes omitted.

had not valued learning, logic, wit, and judgment.

He was not, to be sure, a closet thinker, and distrusted men who were—especially if they preached the Jacobin heresy. For intellect divorced from tradition and experience, as for intellect divorced from conviction and morality, he had all the horror of Burke or Adams. The "ideologue" or "empiric" was, in his judgment, almost as dangerous a man as the obscurantist, and he never tried of berating "those political doctors whose sagacity disdains the admonitions of experimental instruction," whose minds had fallen prey to "too great abstraction and refinement," and "who, enveloped all their lives in the midst of theory, are constantly seeking for an ideal perfection. . . ."

Whatever else he was, Hamilton was neither an ideologue nor an obscurantist. He was, in company with most of the Founding Fathers, a thinking man who read the Great Books, reflected upon his rich experience, and tried his best to arrive at conclusions that were reasonable as well as verifiable, that drew support alike from the speculations of Aristotle, Locke, and Hume and from the behavior of, say, Madison, Washington, Clinton, Burr, and Samuel Chase. He was motivated throughout his mature years by a political philosophy that was never fully articulated but always strongly held. This philosophy was his servant, yet he was also its ward. He could put it to flexible use in political combat, and even, on occasion, put it aside. As he warned one of his followers who insisted upon standing flatly on a "general principle. . .of political economy" (which Hamilton had doubtless taught him), it is often "very important to relax in theory, so as to accomplish as much as may be practicable." Yet he knew perfectly well when, as man

of action and passion, he ignored or stretched or overstepped a fundamental of his philosophy. I think it entirely fair to say that Hamilton was as much governed by general principles as was Adams, Madison, or Jefferson. No doctrinaire, he was nonetheless a man of doctrine. . . .

The fact is, and it is of the highest importance for an understanding of Hamilton's political science, that he believed in the law of nature as a living presence. He may have been fuzzy about definitions and details, especially about the sanctions and sources of the higher law; he may have called too piously upon this law to bless his own endeavors; the "clear voice of natural justice" that spoke to him did not speak quite as clearly to his opponents of the moment, whether Tory apologists or Republican stalwarts or Federalist mavericks. Yet this is only to say that he was a child of his time and place, a man driven by nature and nurture, as was his every friend and every enemy (probably even Burr!), to seek amid the turmoil of events for an ordered pattern of values, to identify this pattern with the notion of a timeless and universal justice, and then to relate himself and his aspirations to it. He was certain that men of good will could listen thoughtfully to the "dictates of reason and equity," and thus learn a little more in each generation of the "great principles of social right, justice and honor." He was certain, too, that free and popular government could not exist for long in contempt of these principles, that a broad commitment to pursue them in a spirit of fundamental decency marked "the essential distinction between free and arbitrary governments. . . ."

Hamilton's dedication to both morality and the moral law had strong if hardly imperious religious overtones. Once again in company with most men of his generation, he thought it inconceivable that "national morality" could be "maintained in exclusion of religious principles"— "morality," he wrote, "*must* fall with religion"—and he found the ultimate source of the commands of natural justice in a "supreme intelligence, who rules the world, and has established laws to regulate the actions of his creatures." He was not a man of deep religious conviction. He was, as far as we can tell, a believing Christian who felt no urge to probe beneath the surface of polite belief. Neither an enthusiast nor a deist, neither a fountain of piety nor a torrent of skepticism, he left questions of religious belief to other men more anxious or qualified to discuss them. While he seems to have been confident in the existence of a God who would sit in benevolent judgment upon him, he was not much more certain than was Jefferson of any other reliable truth about Him. In any case, he seems to have anticipated tens of thousands of later American politicians by being more interested in the social than in the spiritual implications of organized religion. If he was horrified, as Jefferson was not, by the assault upon religion in Jacobin France, his horror was more sociological than theological in character. Atheism was wicked because it denied the existence of God, but even more wicked because it bred anarchy and disorder, and threatened "the subversion of civilized society." Religion was good because it was true, but even better because it was the rock of ordered freedom and, to be quite honest, the custodian of morality among the less educated classes. Hamilton's late (and unfortunate) proposal of a "Christian constitutional Society" would have put Christ to work for the Constitution rather than the Constitution for Christ.

As a final touch to this quick portrait of Hamilton as Whig, we should note that he put abundant trust in "reason" and "experience" as the chief guides to personal conduct, social decision, and moral progress. Like the English masters of the school of natural law, Hamilton would have denied the existence of any sharp conflict between these two ways of knowing and deciding. When he appealed to reason, as he did from time to time, he had in mind what we would call Aristotelian reason—reason applied within the limits of history, facts, and human nature. When he appealed to experience, "the least fallible guide of human opinions," as he did all the time, he had in mind what we would call digested experience—experience appraised with the aid of critical intelligence. And when he appealed to both in the same breath, as he did when he was feeling especially sure of his position, he had in mind nothing less than the great law of nature. The commands of this law could be understood by men who used their powers of reason; its truth was revealed in the "common sense and common practice of mankind." For Hamilton, as for all the men of his generation, experience was the test of reason and reason the interpreter of experience, and both together were the highest source of political wisdom. His constant search was for "solid conclusions, drawn from the natural and necessary progress of human affairs," and it is testimony of the lasting power of the Lockean dispensation that he thought of his own major conclusions as at least crude approximations of the dictates of the law of nature. . . .

Almost every political philosopher worth his salt is first of all a psychologist, a man who shapes his descriptions of social reality and prescriptions for political sanity to a core of assumptions about the urges, needs, habits, and capacities of men. Generalizations about something called "human nature" flow impulsively from his pen, and he seeks everywhere—in history, personal experience, tables of statistics, medical lore, even in the writings of poets and theologians—for evidence to support them.

Hamilton was no exception to this rule. Indeed, it would be hard to find a working and thinking politician in his generation, except perhaps John Adams, who talked more about principles of human behavior, or was more certain that these principles fixed the limits within which the arts of governing could be practiced. . . .

. . .At the risk of bringing too much order to the most disordered area of Hamilton's political science, let me reduce the many convictions he held about human nature to five major themes.

The first is well known to all readers of *The Federalist:* the universal, enduring depravity and frailty of men. Even in the most sanguine days of his life, as an undergraduate enlisted in the glorious cause of the Revolution, he refused to be soft-headed about his fellow men, and thus doused his audience with the cold water of Hume:

"Political writers (says a celebrated author) have established it as a maxim, that, in contriving any system of government, and fixing the several checks and controls of the constitution, *every man* ought to be supposed a *knave.* . . . It is therefore a just *political* maxim, that *every man must be supposed a knave.*"

Never in all his writings, never in all his doings, did Hamilton indulge in the Pelagian dream of the perfectibility of men, nor even in the Jeffersonian dream of amelioration. "The depravity of mankind, in all countries and at all times," was his relentless theme, and he did not even imagine that the improvement of social conditions might give a lasting boost upward to the general level of human conduct. Not "till the millenium comes," and perhaps not even then, would men break loose from the bonds of wickedness and weakness that nature had laid upon them in common.

Among the specific varieties of "natural depravity" that might occasionally take command of even the best of men, including presumably Alexander Hamilton and George Washington, were hatred, cruelty, envy, dishonesty, hypocrisy, treachery, avarice, and bellicosity. He was particularly insistent upon the power of the last of these unfortunate traits. As he demonstrated in *The Federalist,* he had a rather sophisticated grasp of the causes of war, but he always found the first cause to be the rapacious and vindictive nature of men. "The seeds of war are sown thickly in the human breast," he warned those of his countrymen who looked forward to enduring peace.

Hamilton did not always paint his impressionistic pictures of human nature in dark and forbidding colors. "The Supposition of universal venality in human nature," he wrote with feeling in *The Federalist,* "is little less an error in political reasoning than the supposition of universal rectitude." Depravity was a powerful but not omnipotent presence in the community. As he said in 1788 in defending the character of the future Congress of the United States against charges of easy corruptibility, "Human nature must be a much more weak and despicable thing than I apprehend it to be if two hundred of our fellow-citizens can be corrupted in two years." If this is not the most handsome compliment ever paid to the human race, it does show him in his usual frame of mind—"a man disposed to view human nature as it is, without either flattering its virtues or exaggerating its vices."

Like the implicitly loyal Whig he was, Hamilton found man a mixture of degrading vices, discouraging imperfections, and ennobling virtues. "Human conduct," he wrote, "reconciles the most glaring opposites." While the last of these categories was the weakest by far in the characters of all but a few extraordinary men, virtue did exist in most breasts, and it had a way of bursting forth at the most unexpected moments. At one point or another in his writings Hamilton spoke hopefully of honor, generosity, bravery, humaneness, love of liberty, desire for learning, and the sense of justice; and he knew from experience that there were situations in which "human nature" could be made to "rise above itself."

In those great revolutions which occasionally convulse society, human nature never fails to be brought forward in its brightest as well as in its blackest colors.

Yet if Hamilton had a Whiggish belief in the mixed nature of man, he was one of those Whigs like John Adams who found the mixture to be overloaded with vice and folly. Not only was wickedness more deeply planted than goodness in the human breast; it had a way of asserting itself with unusual vigor. "It is a common observation," Hamilton wrote as Phocion in 1784, "that men, bent upon mischief, are more active in the pursuit of their object than those who aim at doing good."

Although he attached great importance to the everlasting tension between well-armed vice and frail virtue in the character of men, Hamilton seems to have believed that three others traits or drives—of an essentially neutral moral nature—were dominant in directing social behavior. Borrowing alike from Hume's *Treatise of Human Nature* and Adam Smith's *Theory of Moral Sentiments*, and relying as always on the lessons he could draw from his own experience, he made much in his own writings of three consuming "loves"—of esteem, of gain, and of power.

The third of Hamilton's major convictions about human nature centered upon the idea of "interest." He never tired of pointing out that every man was, in one important sense, a self-contained unit in the social structure whose first obligation was to himself. He described "self-preservation" respectfully as the "first principle of our nature," "self-love" ironically as an "indispensable duty," "self-interest" coldly as the "most powerful incentive of human actions." Every man had his "interests," whether in gain, esteem, power, pleasure, or simply survival, and there was not much point in telling him that he ought to pursue them in a spirit of moderation and with an eye out for the interests of others. "We may preach," he wrote, "till we are tired of the theme, the necessity of disinterestedness in republics, without making a single proselyte." Having noted already the young Hamilton's approving use of Hume's warning that "*every man* ought to be supposed a *knave*," we may now observe that Hume went on, still with Hamilton's approval, to describe his "everyman" as having "no other end in all his actions, but private interest." While Hamilton, contrary to his own advice, did a fair share of preaching "the necessity of disinterestedness," he based almost all his political calculations on the assumption that he had not made a "single proselyte."

I say "almost" because Hamilton occasionally relaxed the rigidity of his stance as political psychologist and acknowledged the existence of a handful of men to whom the laws of human nature seemed to apply imperfectly or not at all. Having admitted to his colleagues at Philadelphia that "there may be in every government a few choice spirits" who could rise above interest and passion and "act from more worthy motives," he went on some months later in *The Federalist* to rest his case for a strong executive at least partly on the assumption that men of "stern virtue," "men who could neither be distressed nor won into a sacrifice of their duty," would be available for service. While such men were, to be sure, "the growth of few soils," they did exist in sufficient numbers in the United States for the friends of ordered liberty to count upon their presence in the new government. They were evidence of the existence of a "portion of virtue and honor among mankind"; they provided "a reasonable foundation of confidence" in the outcome of the American gamble in freedom. Hamilton did not pause to explain just how the voters, men laden with the average burden of fallibility and envy, could be persuaded to elect men of stern virtue to office. Yet he seemed to have confidence, not as strong as Jefferson's but strong enough to raise his hopes for liberty, that the machinery of election and appointment would throw up enough such men to give a tone of virtue and wisdom to the whole enterprise. . . .

Since reason is largely a product of nurture and passion a product of nature, the latter generally holds the upper hand—"Passion wrests the helm from reason"—and even "wise and good men" are led to the "wrong side of questions of the first magnitude to society" by the "numerous. . .and powerful causes which serve to give a false bias to the judgment." Like most men, including most famous political thinkers, Hamilton found himself to be a man of reason and his critics men of passion, yet this evi-

dence of his own frailty should not obscure the essential candor of one of the constant themes of his declamations on mankind.

Finally, Hamilton insisted that the bad side of human nature, always in a position of natural superiority in its contests with the good, was put in an even more commanding position by the fact of human association. Men in groups, especially groups unrestrained by law or custom, behaved worse than men on their own. "There is a contagion in example," he noted sorrowfully in *The Federalist*, "which few men have sufficient force of mind to resist," and in the nature of things most examples of human behavior were sure to be degrading rather than uplifting. . . .

We may conclude this survey of Hamilton's psychology by noting that he listed a sound knowledge of human nature among the qualifications for lawgivers, especially those who set themselves the task of writing a fundamental law for free men. Somehow the vices of these free men must be brought under control, somehow their virtues must be encouraged, somehow their "loves" must be directed toward healthy ends, somehow their powers of reason must be fortified for the endless duel with prejudice and passion. Most important of all—and here we come close to the core of Hamilton's "science of policy"—their interests must be looked after, secured, if possible gratified, and thus enlisted in the service of the whole community. Again and again in the crucial debates of his public career Hamilton fell back upon this "axiom of political science," which taught him, even if it apparently did not teach men like Jefferson, that the interests of governors and governed alike could be made to "coincide with their duty.". . . .

No accusation we can level against

Hamilton for being a Samaritan toward the rich and a Levite toward the poor can detract from the authority of his message to all makers and manipulators of constitutions: men have interests; these interests govern their comings and goings; government must look to these interests and enlist them in the cause of order, prosperity, and progress. One may argue with Hamilton's identification of the principal interests of the community, or fault him for having enlisted them too lavishly, but one must admit that he put his finger on a fact of political life to which all successful American politicians have paid implicit homage. It is his peculiar merit as political thinker to have been refreshingly explicit in his many references to this first principle of his political science. It was his peculiar merit as political actor to have exploited this principle to build up the Union. One consideration which, so he acknowledged, convinced him of "the expediency of assuming the State debts" was "its tendency to strengthen our infant government by increasing the number of ligaments between the government and the interests of individuals." Rarely has it been given to an American statesman to act so directly upon a fundamental of his political philosophy.

Hamilton's opinions about society had the same style as his opinions about men: dispersed and yet consistent, intuitive and yet thoughtful, offhand and yet highly serviceable. His thinking was always oriented toward society rather than individuals, toward the public welfare rather than the private pursuit of happiness. The community as something more than the men who made it up was an inarticulate major premise of his political creed, and we may acclaim him as one of the first and most conspicuous *social* thinkers on the American scene. If he was not a full-blooded collectivist in his analysis of society, he was most certainly a man who had the higher purposes and claims of the community in full view. He had, moreover, a feeling for the community as an aggregate of men who had a "common national sentiment" and a "uniformity of principles and habits." A "heterogeneous compound" was not his idea of a healthy society. While variety was essential to a healthy social order, it needed a consensus on which to focus.

Like most men with a bias toward society and a way from the individual, Hamilton seems to have thought of the community, perhaps more wishfully than analytically, as a working equilibrium of groups, interests, classes, even estates, each of which drew strength and support from all the others. He was, for example, almost pathetic in his insistence that "the aggregate prosperity of manufactures and the aggregate prosperity of agriculture are intimately connected.". . .

One wishes that Hamilton had been a little more candid, or simply concerned, about the social strata of the young Republic. It may be noted that he acknowledged, without regret, the existence of social classes, and assumed, also without regret, that they would go on forever; that he, like most men of his generation (and of every American generation before and since), made economic achievement and possession the chief criterion of status; that he thought of society as a whole series of layers, yet could not resist the urge to reduce all these layers to two, "the *few* and the *many*," the "rich and wellborn" and "the mass of the people;" and that he betrayed, so far as one can tell, not the slightest interest in the middle class. He might have agreed with Adams, for whom this was a major theme, that the middle class was "that great and excellent portion of society upon whom so much of the liberty and prosperity of nations so greatly depends." He might have been persuaded by his mentor Hume to acknowledge that the "middling rank of men. . .are the best and firmest basis of public liberty." But he never did, and one is left with the feeling that he was essentially a prisoner, and a willing one at that, of the ancient habit of dividing all men simply into the few and the many.

For these few, of course, he had a deep-seated concern. While he was once again casual about a point that Adams, and even Jefferson on occasion, labored forcefully and in detail, Hamilton was as certain as they were that every healthy community nourished a "natural aristocracy" of virtue and talent, and he was a good deal more willing than either of them to identify it with the visible aristocracy of wealth and birth. I have spoken already of his confidence in the existence of "a few choice spirits," and will add only that he expected these spirits somehow to be propelled to the top of the political structure, there to exercise benevolent rule by command, persuasion, and example. I agree unreservedly with Professor Miller that Hamilton "held the 'great man' view of history," that he "tended to glorify the hero, the great state builders, the daring and farsighted who had brought order out of chaos and raised nations to the pinnacle of power," and will add only that he also held, with few reservations, the "great man" theory of politics. For a nation-builder who knew himself rather well, and who had worked in harness with George Washington, it was not unnatural to believe in "the agency of personal considerations in the production of great national events." In his view, the success of popular government depended largely on the commitment of affairs to the "management of disinterested, discreet, and temperate

rulers." The rulers, in turn, would find the support they needed in "the generality of considerate men," in "those whom I call," as he put it to Washington, "the soberminded men of the country.". . .

Whether he looked at the United States through the eyes of tradition or of imagination, he saw a community in which even a rough sort of equality of status and possession among its citizens was an idle dream. Lacking the admirable talent for self-delusion about the fact of social equality displayed by men like John Taylor of Caroline, Hamilton acknowledged both the existence and the staying power of social and economic distinctions. Even if all the unequal privileges inherited from a less rational past were to be wiped away at one stroke, a new inequality would assert itself sooner or later—in a free society, sooner rather than later. He insisted that one of the certain fruits of liberty was inequality—in the first instance inequality of property and thus, in the second instance, inequality of power, consideration, and privilege. Madison records Hamilton as having reminded the Convention that "nothing like an equality of property existed; that an inequality would exist as long as liberty existed, and that it would unavoidably result from that very liberty itself." And Yates records him as having added that "commerce and industry" would "increase the disparity" of property "already great among us."

Since Hamilton was a true believer in the benefits of commerce and industry and at least a modest advocate of the uses of liberty, one must describe him as a man unwilling to sacrifice the prosperity and glory of the nation on the altar of a specious dedication to equality. He never went out of his way, as did Adams in his own generation and Calhoun in the next, to applaud the distribution of "unequal portions" of virtue and talent among men, but he would doubtless have agreed with them that inequality was a major spur of progress in all the affairs of mankind. While he professed a Whiggish belief in "the sublime idea of a perfect equality of rights among citizens," he was not prepared to give the operative word "rights" an expansive definition. While he took pains to tell Jefferson in 1791 (who took pains to commit it to writing "in the moment of A.H.'s leaving the room") that a "mind must be really depraved which would not prefer the equality of political rights which is the foundation of pure republicanism," he added at once the critical qualification— "if it can be obtained consistent with order." Equity, not equality, was the last notable mark of Hamilton's good society. Each man deserved his due, but what was due to any two men was, in the total view of their rights, not exactly the same. When he said to the Convention "that every individual of the community at large has an equal right to the protection of government," he meant only to say that the laws must not discriminate wilfully among classes or interests or sections. That these differences among men would and should exist, that they were differences of status and influence as well as of vocation and property, and that they should be protected against the rage for leveling were all fundamentals of Hamilton's social thought. . . .

Hamilton the social thinker was an interesting blend of the "pluralist," the "dualist," and the "unitarian." The last of these approaches to the study of society was, I think, ascendant in his philosophy. Sometimes he seems to have been most impressed with the diversity of groups and classes in the community, and concerned to discover and adjust the delicate balance of forces among them; other times he was more impressed with the way in which all men could divide, at least for political purposes, into "the few" and "the many," and concerned to give each of these mighty forces the most suitable weapons for the struggle. But almost always he was most impressed with the community itself, and concerned to discover the terms of the higher unity into which, he was certain, all men and groups and classes must finally merge. Throughout his life, in every medium and on every occasion, he stated his belief in the existence of "the public interest." So strong was this belief, so often did he fall back upon it for inspiration, that one historian of American political thought has labeled him the "Rousseau of the Right." Although the equation of Hamilton's belief in an overriding public interest with Rousseau's theory of the General Will raises more questions than it answers, it does point up the streak of political Romanticism that ran all through this area of his thought.

Hamilton's favorite label for the common interest that transcends all private interests was "the public good," a phrase much loved by the leading men of his generation and easily discovered in the treasure house of political thought, notably in Hume's political essays. . . .

The most serious question one is forced to ask is whether Hamilton was not in fact caught up in a fundamental inconsistency that a more penetrating or simply more patient mind could have recognized and then resolved: the inconsistency between a view of politics, which he held in moments of idealism, that focused upon something great and noble called "the public good," and a view of politics, upon which he fell back in moments of realism, that focused upon something tenacious and seminal called "private interests." Now there is no doubt that this inconsistency lay deep in his political consciousness, and that he never made a final choice of one view or the other as the core around which to group all his other insights and assumptions about society. There is also no doubt that his mind was caught in the middle of an undeclared (and thus unacknowledged) war between the consequences of these views, and that as a result he is a something less than satisfactory exponent of the theory of social interests. Yet it is probable that his attempt to have it both ways—to celebrate the splendors of the public good and exhort men to honor it, to acknowledge the primacy of private interests and expect men to pursue them—was the mark not of a mind too confused to see that a choice must be made or too weak to make it, but of a mind honest enough to reflect the tension in the community itself between the needs that each man shares with all other men and the needs he shares with only a few men or even with none at all.

One cannot help but think that Hamilton did the right thing intellectually—by which I mean that he kept his thoughts in touch with reality—when he paid equal respect, if never equal homage, to the public good and, as a social force not exactly identical with it, to the sum of all the private goods. If he was confused and contradictory, so, too, was the reality of the society for which he was hoping to lay down a few effective rules of decision. Is there not, he would have a right to ask his critics, a public good that envelops the common and long-range interests of the community and of every man in it? Is there not also a vast array of groups and personal interests that poses a constant threat to the public good? And are there not ways—prizes, penalties, examples, threats, incantations, customs—to make each man conscious of the public

good, to persuade him of his own stake in it, to teach him the limits of pursuit of his private interests, and, most important, to create a situation in which even a selfish attention to these interests will perhaps strengthen the public good?

Hamilton always insisted that there were such ways, and one must admire his tenacity in refusing to give up the search for a workable pattern of popular government in which, as he told his friends in Philadelphia, laws and rulers "availed" themselves of the passions and interests of men "in order to make them subservient to the public good." It must always be his distinction that he, more pointedly than any other political thinker of his time, introduced the concept of the public good into American thought. Because of the inherent complexity of the concept and the shotgun methods of the conceiver, the introduction was certain to be confusing. Yet if a Romantic named Rousseau is celebrated for having confused us with his vague idea of a General Will, a Romantic named Hamilton can be admired for having confused us with his vague idea of a Public Good. There are those who argue that the first duty of the political scientist is to throw thinking men into studied confusion, and both Rousseau and Hamilton did this duty with a vengeance.

Hamilton's simultaneous celebration of the public good and deference to private interests goes far to explain his ambivalent yet basically censorious attitude toward political parties, which is most clearly revealed in his draft of the Farewell Address. On one hand, he knew that associations of like-minded men for political purposes were bound to arise in a free society, and he admitted that parties, when they were doing their best, might provide "salutary checks upon the administration of the government" and "invigorate the spirit of liberty." On the other, he had a low opinion of their "best," and no opinion at all of their will to do it, and would gladly have looked forward to a future without them. Like most men of his time, he had given no real thought to these still formless phenomena. He never made room in his political science for a theory of political parties because he never imagined them as fully developed, essential, both dynamic and stabilizing adjuncts of the political process. To the end of his life he refused to believe that the party he led was a party at all. It was, rather, a kind of *ad hoc* committee of correspondence of men with a large view of America's destiny, a rudimentary instrument of the public good that had been reluctantly created by him and his friends to meet the wrongheaded challenge of men like Clinton and Jefferson.

The truth is that he identified "party" with "faction," and defined "faction" simply as a "small number" of men "inimical to the common voice" of the country. Hobbes had told him that a faction was "as it were a city in a city," and such an image was deeply disturbing to this advocate of the public good. Hume had told him that "factions subvert government, render laws impotent, and beget the fiercest animosities among men of the same nation, who ought to give mutual assistance and protection to each other," and this self-conscious builder of a nation agreed that "founders of factions" ought therefore to be "detested and hated." Faction was simply private interest writ large; it was the passions and ambitions of a self-regarding group of men in hostile array against "the good of the whole community." Factions, by definition, were vehicles of particular interests, and the clash of faction with faction would too often do damage to the public interest. All in all, he was forced to

conclude, the "spirit of faction" was the "bane of free government" and the "mortal poison of our land," faction itself a "demon" of "pestilential breath," not least because it represented the challenge of a selfish minority to the large majority. The notion of faction as majority seems never to have occurred to him. As he put the matter rhetorically but honestly at the time of the Whiskey Rebellion:

Shall the majority govern or be governed? shall the nation rule or be ruled? shall the general will prevail, or the will of a faction? shall there be government or no government?

In Hamilton's political science, "faction" and "party" were two labels for the same political phenomenon, and it was a phenomenon to strike fear into the hearts of all friends of orderly self-government. "Sedition and party rage," "petulance of party," "rage of party spirit," "unaccommodating spirit of party," "delirium of party spirit," "rage of party," "baneful spirit of party," "cant phrases of party," "heats of party," "that intolerant spirit which has at all times characterized political parties"—these were plainly the words of a man who did not imagine that parties, as he knew them or perhaps even as we know them, could be useful instruments in the political process, who meant what he said when, in a typical burst of political Romanticism, he told the Poughkeepsie Convention that "we are attempting by this Constitution to abolish factions and to unite all parties for the general welfare." Even if we discount his natural propensity to call any group of men who opposed his plans for the nation a "faction," we must conclude that his belief in the essentially malevolent influence of self-willed minorities extended to almost all political groupings in the community. For a man who was one of the first and most explicit to direct attention to the tenacious power of private interests, he was strangely reluctant to make a full place in his political science for the concerted pursuit of these interests by groups of like-minded men. He should have been persuaded by his own wisdom in such matters that this pursuit was a natural agency of free government; he could never rid himself of the assumption that it was a "natural disease.". . .

ADRIENNE KOCH (1912-   ), professor of history at the University of Maryland, is a leading student of the American Enlightenment. In a series of books, she has sympathetically explored the ideas of Jefferson and Madison, relating them to the European Enlightenment and contrasting them with the views of their American opponents. In the following selection, she studies the political thought of James Madison, "Father of the Constitution" and a founder of the Republican party. By comparing Madison's ideas with Hamilton's, one can perceive more clearly the ideological differences that generated party development and why Republican doctrine proved to be more popular than Federalist doctrine. °

James Madison and the Politics of Republicanism

America demands bold lines and strong personalities in its public men. It might almost be said that unless a man lends himself to caricature he will not be included in the company of American political greats. James Madison has accordingly suffered unduly at the hands of American historians, and he has suffered even more in being denied an appropriate place in the affections of the American people. For my own part, I should like to confess that I took for granted the prevailing attitude about Madison, as in every way the junior lieutenant to Jefferson, when I first began my studies of the American philosopher-statesman. It was with genuine surprise that I gradually came to realize that this gentle and modest man was not the pure scholar who had wandered into politics, there to be given favors of office by the great Republican leader with whom he was closely associated. He was. . .in every way a full collaborator with Jefferson in forming the Republican Party and in developing that Republican ideology which is still unmatched in the modern theory of democracy. He was also the amalgamator of all the essential elements in the Republican tradition, conceived in the broad sense; for he achieved, in his thought and character, a total balance among Jef-

°Adrienne Koch, *Power, Morals and the Founding Fathers*, Chapter VI. © 1961 by Cornell University. Used by permission of Cornell University Press. Footnotes omitted.

ferson's ideals for the pursuit of happiness, Hamilton's understanding of strategic means, and Adams' realization of the need to check power with power.

In this unique capacity as amalgamator, not only must we acknowledge Madison's contribution in designing the Constitution but we should at last be ready to appreciate the other important aspects of his political genius. Among these are his leadership in the first Congress under the Constitution; his advisory role to President Washington; his great share in the intellectual creation of the political ideals and beliefs of the Republican Party; his major contribution to the organization of that party; his strength as a diplomatist; and his firm and lifelong defense of the vital principles of government by majority rule with minority rights. It is also noteworthy that this even-tempered statesman was so absorbed by the great objects to which he gave himself that he almost never claimed anything for himself as a person, save that he hoped he had been able to make use of the opportunities offered him to advance the happiness of his country "and the hope of the world."

Madison's principles are of unusual interest today for a number of reasons. But one reason is central to all the others—the development and defense of the philosophy of democracy in strategic terms in a world where it is gravely threatened. Madison was an extraordinary scholar who looked to the past for what he could learn about democratic procedures, and who thus prepared himself to become the most informed member of the Constitutional Convention. He looked to the future, to the establishment of a free government which would have enduring power and yet enough flexibility to permit adjustments to new problems in a changing world. Finally, Madison was aware, not only of the value of establishing a long-range policy for the American republic, but also of the significance of the democratic experiment for the future of mankind. He nourished the deep hope that the American experiment would succeed and, in time, become a model for all people. It is in this ultimate bearing of his work and wish that he arrests the attention of the contemporary world; for he disposes us to ask whether our government can provide leadership which other nations can support and follow to maintain a free world against a powerful and aggressive political tyranny.

Madison's pointed message on America's role in the world is contained in an unusual letter which he composed at the close of his life, while in philosophic retirement. He wrote:

The free system of government we have established is so congenial with reason, with common sense, and with a universal feeling, that it must produce approbation and a desire of imitation, as avenues may be found for truth to the knowledge of nations. Our Country, if it does justice to itself, will be the workshop of liberty to the Civilized World, and do more than any other for the uncivilized.

In this revelatory phrase, "workshop of liberty," Madison caught the dynamic meaning of the idea of America. There is an integral connection between Madison's thought of a workshop of liberty and Jefferson's ideal of the pursuit of happiness: first, because the pursuit of happiness involves the work and discipline of free men and, second, because the workshop of liberty makes the pursuit of happiness possible; it is a pre-condition of the happiness that is virtue. Here also we have a recognition of the strategic economic means that protect and advance liberty. Madison saw that the "great and advancing cause of a representative government" must marshal on its side continued prosperity in order to give the people relief from disintegrating sources of poverty and unemployment and in order to make good in fact its promised liberty and happiness.

If we go somewhat deeper into Madison's political philosophy, we will find at its core the function he assigns to power in relation to liberty. Madison constantly defends a political program or policy by showing how it protects, assures, or promotes the cause of liberty. On the other hand, he tries just as earnestly to secure liberty by assuring the appropriate powers necessary for its realization. His work is quite distinctive in its explicit and habitual counterpoising of these two elements, these two conditions necessary for successful free government. Placed in this context, one sees the significance of Madison's early efforts to assure a strong central government as a successor to the weak Confederation, but a government to be based on the sovereignty of the people and with its power limited by various checks and balances.

1

Madison's genius in compromising the opposed claims of power and liberty in the Constitutional Convention hardly requires review. For this role he has been hailed as the "father" of the Constitution. This is reflected in Madison's contribution to the *Federalist Papers*. It is generally recognized that Hamilton and Madison were able to join in this taxing writing enterprise because they had much in common. The two men had played a great role in the continentalist movement behind the Constitution, and the *Federalist Papers* was their joint effort to provide the political rationale that would wrest from the states the all-important ratification. But what is even now but imperfectly realized is that their views were far from identical—that one can, in fact, discriminate two different philosophies of power, the Hamiltonian and the Madisonian. Certain basic assumptions about human nature as relevant to the problem of government are, of course, common to both authors. They agree on what is ordinarily described as a "realist" interpretation of human nature, that men are selfish, more prone to be governed by passion than reason, contentious, capricious, avaricious, and wicked; but they are less united in the degree of emphasis placed upon these qualities. Hamilton, for example, tends to exaggerate the tone of pessimism. He speaks of "the ordinary depravity of human nature," of the fiery and destructive passions of war that reign in the human breast, of "uncontrollable impulses of rage, . . .jealousy, . . .and other irregular and violent propensities." This leads Hamilton to stress a strong central government.

For Madison, on the other hand, the glory of the federative system in the Constitution was its division of power between two distinct governments "and then the portion allotted to each subdivided among distinct and separate departments." He valued this distribution of power because it provided "a double security. . .to the rights of the people. The different governments will control each other, at the same time that each will be controlled by itself."

The outcome of these differences between Hamilton and Madison can be seen in their view on factions. One of the most interesting sentences in Hamilton's writings is his remark in the debate in the New York Convention that "we are attempting by this constitution to abolish factions and to unite all parties for the general welfare." This is not an isolated or unguarded statement but an expression of a consistent belief that the new union, it properly strong, could avoid the troublesomeness of the party system. No view could contrast more markedly with the universe of Madison's tenth *Federalist* article where the existence of factions is taken as the fundamental structural fact of a pluralistic, free society. Not that Madison supposes factions free of danger to society; but, as he says, we cannot cure a disease by killing the patient—cannot, that is, if we care about the patient. Factions for Madison were special-interest groups arising out of the fundamental conflict present in every society between those who are rich and want to maintain their riches and those who are poor and strugggle to relieve their condition. "All civilized societies are divided into different interests and factions," he wrote in the interesting year of 1787, "as they happen to be creditors or debtors—rich or poor—husbandmen, merchants or manufacturers—members of different religious sects—followers of different political leaders—inhabitants of different districts—owners of different kinds of property, etc."

For Madison the great virtue of a republic is to provide that liberty which permits factions to breathe and to provide those internal and external limits on destructive license which encourage reasonable compromise of the multiple conflicting interests. He recognizes diversity, welcomes it, and provides for the kind of order that emerges from compromise and reciprocal controls. He is much concerned on all important questions with what he prudently calls "requisite power" and energy in government, but he invariably joins these necessary means with their proper ends—liberty, justice, and the rights of the people. Madison accordingly considers a republic "the least imperfect" of human governments; he has faith that it "promises the cure for which we are

asking." Such wise tenets play no part in Hamilton's view of factions; the disease must be cured—let the patient beware. Thus, Hamilton's endorsement of the Constitution imperfectly conceals his disbelief: "I am persuaded that it is the best which our political situation, habits and opinions will admit."

The following passage in Number 10 of the *Federalist Papers* reveals the key to Madison's fundamental political thought:

As long as the reason of man continues fallible, and he is at liberty to exercise it, different opinions will be formed. As long as the connection subsists between his reason and his self-love, his opinions and his passions will have a reciprocal influence on each other; and the former will be objects to which the latter will attach themselves. The diversity in the faculties of men, from which the rights of property originate, is not less an insuperable obstacle to a uniformity of interests. The protection of these faculties is the first object of government. From the protection of different and unequal faculties of acquiring property, the possession of different degrees and kinds of property immediately results; and from the influence of these on the sentiments and views of the respective proprietors, ensues a division of the society into different interests and parties.

Madison developed a most important implication of his theory of factions for the support of a federal form of government. Where Hamilton wanted unity and felt that this could only be achieved by a strong central executive, Madison saw the feasibility and desirability of maintaining diversity within the United States. He saw this as being made possible by extending the operational sphere of real factions and by providing for their representation in a federal form of government still responsive to the people. On this ground he was able to reject the prevailing idea of Montesquieu that a

republic required a small extent of territory. He went further and argued that,
with a wide enough extension of territory,
a more effective and durable republic
could be established. For in such an extensive republic, with a multiplication of
different factions and their appropriate
representation, there could be secure interests and safeguards for both the exercise of majority rule and the protection
of minority rights. On these theoretical
grounds Madison was able to advance the
need for a tighter federal union without
requiring either the tyranny of the few or
the tyranny of the majority to make it
work.

2

One is also moved to admire the skill
with which Madison developed his great
theme in a series of papers he wrote for
the *National Gazette* in 1792, defining the
principles to which the Republican Party
pledged adherence—papers that I have
long considered worthy of separate publication and wide distribution for readers
today. One essay on "Consolidation"
described the natural tendency of government to follow a self-directed course
when "the public mind" had no voice or
was apathetic. The only way to counter
such consolidation was to have an alert
citizenry, whose close participation in
local and state governments would permit
them to express "the sense of the people"
on important issues. Madison thought
that the various authorities established by
our unique federal system could be used
to create "one paramount Empire of
reason, benevolence, and brotherly affection." Another paper on "Public
Opinion" declared it to be the agency to
set bounds on every free government. Although Madison had not at first been in
favor of the Bill of Rights, he had come to
see the importance of Jefferson's argu-

ments in its behalf; he had moved their
adoption in the first Congress under the
Constitution, and he now asserted that
declarations of principles and rights had
the important function of influencing
public opinion and thus in turn creating
further pressure in the direction of free
government.

In a succeeding paper called "Liberty
and Power," Madison pointed out that in
Europe charters of liberty had, in some
cases, been granted by established power,
whereas America had introduced a new
practice—to issue "charters of power
granted by liberty." He proposed a
formula for true republicans: "Liberty
against power, and power against licen-
tiousness." In a paper devoted to "Property," Madison distinguished between
two major senses of the term: the first was
the narrow sense, including money, possessions, and the right to exclude others
from the objects we own; the second, the
broad sense, implied that men have "property" in their religious opinions, in the
liberty and safety of their persons, and in
the free use of their physical and mental
faculties. When governments pride themselves on guarding the inviolability of
property, Madison warned, let them see
that they respect the broad property in
rights as well as the narrow rights of property. The summing up, however, Madison reserved for an imaginary dialogue
between a "Republican" and an "anti-
Republican." The latter argues that the
government must be strong above all, the
people submissive. The Republican expos-
tulates, obviously with Hamilton in mind:
"What a perversion of the natural order
of things. . .to make power the primary
and central object of the social system,
and Liberty but its satellite."

In the test by fire which is actual politics rather than political theory, Madison
showed himself strong. He distinguished

himself first by waging a major campaign against Hamilton's proposal to secure public credit without discriminating in favor of the original holders of the debt. These had been forced to part with their securities at desperately low prices because of the impaired credit under the Articles of Confederation, and the present holders, many of whom were speculators, had bought up the certificates in large quantities after they had discovered that the government, under Hamilton, might honor the securities at face value. Madison's appeal for discrimination between these two classes of holders, based on what he considered equitable and humane, did not succeed in changing Hamilton's plan for securing the public debt. But it showed the sincerity of his stated ideals of moral restraints on the use of power, and it was the beginning of a fateful holding action by Republicans against the Federalists and their broad program of power.

The same issue lies at the heart of the famous controversy over the "strict" and "broad" interpretations of the Constitution. Jefferson and Madison, watching the logically progressive steps taken by Hamilton and the Federalists for tightening their grasp on state power, could hardly feel it safe to agree with Hamilton's axiom that "every power vested in a government is in its nature sovereign, and includes. . .a right to employ all the *means* requisite and fairly applicable to the attainment of the ends of such power. . . ." Madison in an important speech to Congress, and Jefferson in a parallel opinion on the constitutionality of the Federal Bank sent to President Washington at his request, both argued that the phrases "to lay taxes to provide for the general welfare" and "to make all laws necessary and proper for carrying into execution the enumerated powers,"

could not be used to reduce the whole Constitution to the single statement that Congress be instituted with power to do whatever would be for the good of the United States. For in that event, Jefferson warned, the administration would be the sole judges of good and evil, and thus in fact they would have the power to do whatever evil they pleased. Madison, who well remembered what had taken place in the Convention, recalled that the proposal to authorize Congress to open canals and incorporate them had been rejected for one reason, because it was feared that Congress might then also have the power to create a bank. In the Convention, Madison had proposed that Congress be empowered to "grant charters of incorporation," but the delegates rejected his suggestion. He interpreted this as the intention to confine Congress to the enumerated powers and to the *indispensable* means to carry the enumerated powers into effect. Apart from the intricate arguments advanced by both sides, there were two substantial issues in conflict. Jefferson and Madison were trying to safeguard the people's liberty from what they were now calling a "money despotism," and they were anxious to protect the states in order to have the states as a countervailing power against further national assumptions of power. Hamilton hoped to carry out, by energetic administration, his original ideal of a strong national government, free from what he called the "depredations" of the states and the untrustworthy common people they might represent.

Some years later, in 1798 and 1799, in a crisis situation, Jefferson and Madison issued famous protests against the oppressive Alien and Sedition Laws passed by the Federalists. These were the "Virginia and Kentucky Resolutions," which effectually discouraged the federal government from ever again attempting to move openly against the freedom of the press. Far more was involved than the dialectic of "states' rights" to which the two authors resorted. They were waging a classic fight to defend civil liberties and to keep alive the two-party system without which only the husk of self-government can remain.

Power, then, in one form or another, is necessary to protect liberty. In simplistic fashion this truth becomes distorted by some people into a naïve cult of efficiency, and grave fears are voiced that democracy is weak because it is less organized than total economies. In this mood Hamilton is revered as the symbol of organizing imagination and managerial power. But people forget that it was no mean business to control Hamilton's power, both in Congress, where his fiscal reports were presented, and in the executive, where his power tended to override that of the other Cabinet members. Madison as leader in Congress and Jefferson as Secretary of State were able to curb Hamilton's power program and thereby assure that the Secretary of the Treasury should not have the full executive powers he tried to assume. This aspect of Jefferson's and Madison's realistic efforts to assure limited powers at the outset of our government is not taken into account by those who worship Hamilton as the realist.

3

Madison developed some basic but not obvious implications of this central position at a remarkably early phase in the development of democratic theory. One aspect happens to be older and much sounder than the one normally accepted as the classic British formulation of liberalism, that of John Stuart Mill. Mill's position tends to posit reason at the center of all democratic procedures and to assume a habit or practice of rationality as characteristic of human nature. This view distorts the actual findings about the human nature in all societies about which we have knowledge. In order to reject such an undue emphasis on reason, one does not have to ground the rejection on the findings of Freud or the sociological derivative formulation in Pareto's theory of nonlogical actions. For it appears that Madison, without benefit of Freud or Pareto, found it possible to establish a realistic position on human nature as the center of his political theory. He held that men were naturally moved by interests and associated passions and would naturally organize themselves to protect and promote these interests. But men could also respond to the appeal of more important and enduring "general interests," especially if they were helped to do so by being denied a monopoly of power! This is the basic significance of Madison's theory of factions.

This theory of factions, as a proper outcome of the workings of human nature in any society, enabled Madison on important occasions in his career to seize strategic opportunities to promote liberty in a realistic setting. In truth, one should understand that it is this conception of strategic opportunities which distinguishes the work of a philosopher-statesman from that of both a political opportunist and a philosopher-king. The opportunist does not function as a principled political leader; he is not committed to serious moral stakes. The philosopher-king is too far removed from a political setting to have any effective bearing on translating ideal outcomes into directed actions and therefore tends to complain about all society and mankind for refusing to be led to the perfect state. Now, Madison had moral goals—the ex-

illusion of liberty, not only here and now but over time and, he hoped, over the earth. For this reason he recognized conflicting interests and the need somehow to resolve and compromise these interests while advancing—not sacrificing—the cause of liberty. His work on the separation of church and state, his concern with the separation of powers, the dual sovereignty envisaged in the Constitution, as well as the time limitations upon holding legislative and executive authority, his ultimate sponsorship of the Bill of Rights, and his tireless defense of the Union after sharp North-South conflict had developed in the last years of his life—all these activities recognized the need to work somehow through factional interests to the common good.

The theory of factions has been seized on as a kind of primitive formulation of the theory of class. But here, too, it is important to recognize Madison's advance not only over Mill but also over Marx. Marx's so-called realism amounts to a denial of ideal motives and the reduction of political and other interests to a class position in the economy. This is clearly a serious distortion of human nature and human behavior—not to say of history. Madison recognized the pervasive character of conflict in all human society and the pervasive drive to improve the conditions of society. Marx felt that he was inheriting the mantle of liberalism by espousing the myth of a *classless* society to succeed all political organizations of states which defend class and, ultimately, economic position. There is, according to Madison's understanding of the *universal* character of factional behavior, no possibility of such a leap from political necessity to social freedom. For Marx, the theory of the classless society may not, apparently, have been intended as a noble lie, nor was it the ignoble lie used in

Communist propaganda as one weapon among others to force men to accept the current state of tyranny. We must credit Madison's political realism with convicting Marx himself of utopian socialism. What is more, it convicts all utopias of serious political error, because they ignore the reality of factions and posit a more perfect state or society than could possibly be realized. Acting on utopian theory can only result in the assumption of arbitrary and ultimately total power to keep intact the utopian citadel, a confectionary citadel concocted out of an unrealistic view of man.

4

Madison's enlightened realism is presented in unforgettable terms in an unaddressed draft of a letter written late in his life. Madison dryly wrote:

No government of human device and human administration can be perfect; . . .that which is the least imperfect is therefore the best government; that the abuses of all other governments have led to the preference of republican governments as the best of all governments, because the least imperfect.

In short, there is no perfect state. The "idealistic" theory that there is one, is likely to lead to a total state, as in Plato or in Marx. But there is a *best state under the given conditions*, and this is one which permits majority rule while protecting minority rights—essentially, the democratic form of government. And there are always possibilities for more democracy. This enables us to distinguish between the failings of a democracy at any one time or place and the negation of democracy altogether. It is not necessary to deny there is Negro discrimination to affirm there is democracy in the United States.

Another implication of Madison's

theory of conjoining power with liberty has some bearing on the current debate on security measures in a democratic society. Power does tend to corrupt, unless it is moved by moral goals and is limited by political safeguards of the kind imposed in the Constitution—regular elections, the separation of powers, and the Bill of Rights, among others. But even then certain interests, when organized politically, may be out to seize power and, when in power, destroy the safeguards for other minorities. Therefore under certain conditions it may be necessary, in order to protect liberty, to use power to prevent such interests from functioning effectively. There is no justification for being so weak as to invite disaster, but there is an exacting obligation to be careful to use only as much power as is necessary to protect liberty. Obviously, conditions will vary at any one time as to whether more or less power is required for this purpose. There will be differences about the extent of the power needed to combat present evils. By the same logic, however, there may be opportunities, for those not moved by moral ends, to seize upon changed situations to strengthen their own power. The guide for Madison in this complex nexus of power and liberty is similar to the guide for Justice Holmes, the test of a "clear and present danger"; and this standard must take into account whether avenues to reason have been kept relatively open or have been blocked.

Two further aspects of the theory of factions in relation to democratic governments are pertinent to contemporary problems. Both these aspects have to do with Madison's belief that the American republic was likely to be more successful than previous experiments because it would be an "extensive" republic. Extension, for Madison, involved the multiplication of factions on the probability that, with the ways open for debate and public discussion, plus the political safeguards established in the Constitution, no one faction would be overwhelming.

We see factions today, organized on a national scale, exercising their influence to secure their self-interest. Yet they do not preclude the coexistence of other factions—in part because they are not overwhelming and in part because they are not wholly unified as a single faction. Agriculture, labor, and business exert combined pressures on the government. The people must choose their government in the light of the issues and programs sponsored by these factions and by other pressure groups, as they are reflected in party platforms and legislative proposals. Clearly, we all need agriculture, labor, and business, and consequently there is no convenient wholesale solution for ridding ourselves of these special interests. There is no doubt that serious national problems have been created by parity pricing, monopolistic labor organizations, or monopolistic business interests and influences. For these reasons our future success as a democracy depends in large part on the wisdom we cultivate in compromising, balancing, and resolving these special interests to promote the cause of liberty. This is one aspect of Madison's theory of factions that has meaning today.

The other aspect of the extensive republic and the multiplication and diffusion of factions concerns Madison's hope that our form of government might function as an inspirational model for the rest of the world. An extensive republic that is best for man, not in being perfect but in being least imperfect, is one that moves toward a world government. This is, so to speak, the goal of man's efforts to use the power he can create to secure peace and freedom. This, in a sense, is the secular equivalent of "peace on earth to men of good will." Drawing up exquisite blueprints of ideal societies or perfect constitutions cannot bring us one step nearer to the goal, nor can the wild suggestion of preventive war set us on the path. Madison's strategy is the only one potentially useful in moving us in this direction. It would imply organizing workable federations of united states where there are joint needs and where tolerable procedures for solving factional issues can be established.

The problems of Western Europe may look hopeless to many today, but so did those of the states under the Articles of Confederation. It was the recognition of strong mutual interests, the spur of self-preservation, and the cogent and disinterested leadership of great Americans that made the Constitutional Convention a success. Europe today may appear to have unsolvable and irreconcilable problems. But there are mutual interests: there is the increasing spur of self-preservation; and there are indications among Europeans of the need for disinterested leadership. And here Madison's hope for the role of America as a catalyst in organizing more extensive republics is not only morally compelling but may perhaps function as a practical guide.

5

In his time Madison made himself a critic of the kind of institutionalized religion that claimed to have rights over all men to force its particular brand of faith. He affirmed the national right to religious belief along the path which a free conscience has chosen. The source of his faith was a love of man expressed by devotion to the real and solid condition that could encourage men to be fully human—the universal recognition of the equal rights of men to be free, to govern themselves as

best they could, to better their physical, social, mental, and spiritual life. Cherishing this faith as one that could unite men and constitute, in effect, a common faith, Madison repudiated every attempt by religious organizations to obtain control in the political domain. For one who sincerely cultivated the equal rights of men, only a republican setting where men would be free to worship—or even not to worship—was fitting. In his own day, therefore, Madison succeeded in the Virginia legislature in establishing religious freedom and separating church and state. He extended this position in the Constitutional Convention and repeated his success in the First Congress by moving for the introduction of the Bill of Rights.

This insistence upon the purely private dimension of religious worship and its attendant warning against any attempted church invasion of the state is familiar to anyone who knows the early history of this country. But it is necessary, nevertheless, to call attention to it today because in our opposition to Communist power there is a tendency to seek some other total salvation. It is right, in Madison's terms, to attack the Communist philosophy as a false totalitarian faith, one which denies the natural rights of man. But there is, according to the founding fathers, no justification for forcing the belief that there is one and only one true religion for all, by which all other ways of life and belief are to be cried down as false and wiped out.

By this, as indeed by all his hard struggles, Madison was declaring his great faith in the uniqueness of the American system, that "federative" system which he loved and proudly described as "itself not a little experimental. . . . It not only excites emulation without enmity, but admits local experiments of every sort, which, if failing, are but a partial and temporary evil; if successful, may become a common and lasting improvement." This was the Madison who had ruefully reflected in the *Federalist Papers* that men were not angels and that government itself is "the greatest of all reflections of human nature. If men were angels, no government would be necessary. If angels were to govern men, neither external nor internal controls on government would be necessary." By such realistic judgments accompanied by a generous faith in man, Madison was recommending, I would think, the positive encouragement of variety in unity. No one religion, he saw, could unite society or mankind—one political state, or way of life, or mental set. Yet all men could have one common faith, as common as their existence as natural animals, as common as their need for air, for food, for movement from place to place, for borrowing and improving each other's ideas. That faith—one that could spread by exciting "emulation without envy," that experiment that would touch off similar but not identical experiments, that growing unity that could be worked from the most diverse materials—that was the faith in the natural rights of man. It was and is a powerful faith, that none monopolize, no

nation owns, and no one can be diminished by.

We can easily understand how one who had translated such a high faith into a unique political experiment, a "workshop of liberty," would take pride, as he looked back over a half-century, that "the ark" had survived. Such deeply engrained hopes and love moved Madison to leave a last message to his countrymen—a message which has assuredly not lost its meaning for our divided world. This message solemnly states:

As this advice, if it ever see the light will not do it till I am no more, it may be considered as issuing from the tomb, when the truth alone can be respected, and the happiness of man alone consulted. It will be entitled therefore to whatever weight can be derived from good intentions, and from the experiences of one who has served his country in various stations through his life to the cause of its liberty and who has borne a part in most of the transactions which will constitute epochs of its destiny.

The advice nearest to my heart and deepest in my convictions is that the Union of the States be cherished and perpetuated. Let the open enemy to it be regarded as a Pandora with her box opened; and the disguised one, as the serpent creeping with his deadly wiles into Paradise.

Political parties formalized the conduct of politics by creating relatively permanent organizational structures to mobilize the electorate. Candidates no longer relied on haphazard efforts to produce victory at the polls, because partisans discovered that success often hinged on methodical arrangements. The more competitive party politics were, the greater was the incentive and necessity to persuade, register, cajole, and bring out the voters. In the following essay, CARL E. PRINCE (1934-   ), of Seton Hall University, examines the development of the Republican organization in New Jersey, describing both its internal structure and the groups from which it recruited leadership and cadre. This study is part of a larger study of New Jersey's Jeffersonian Republicans.°

The Development of a Party Machine

Investigations in the last decade or so have shed much light on the evolution of party machinery in the period of the Federalists and Democratic-Republicans. These studies have picked up where George Luetscher left off more than sixty years ago. In their quest for an understanding of the origins and growth of party machinery in the United States, recent students of party politics have focused particularly on the Democratic-Republican party, and they have often conducted their inquiries at the state level, producing detailed and accurate accounts of the early stages in the development of political machinery.

Many of these studies, past and present, have provided instructive insights into party patronage as it appeared in the Republican party after 1800, but they have, in turn, raised and left unanswered a number of questions about patronage. It is clear, for instance, that there was widespread distribution of state offices to deserving Republicans in some states both before and after Jefferson became President in 1801, and that beginning in 1801 federal patronage became important to the party. What remains unclear is the precise identity of the "deserving" and to what extent active Republican party workers were rewarded for their political

°Carl E. Prince, "Patronage and a Party Machine: New Jersey Democratic-Republican Activists, 1801-1816," *William and Mary Quarterly*, XXI (Oct. 1964), pp. 571-578. Reprinted by permission of the Institute of Early American History, Williamsburg, Virginia. Footnotes omitted.

efforts. In short, the question is whether the available patronage was systematically used to strengthen the local Republican machine.

This study attempts to answer this question for New Jersey in the years 1801-16. It does not contend that New Jersey's experience with party patronage in this period was typical. Any such contention must await further researches into the operation of political machinery in other states. In any event, in New Jersey a highly organized and effective patronage machine, run by and for active party workers, went into operation soon after the Republican party captured the state for the first time in 1801. The Republicans remained in power from 1801 until 1816, with only two exceptions: in 1802 the legislature was evenly divided, and in 1812 the Federalists regained control of the state government for a year.

During their hegemony, the Democratic-Republicans constructed a sound party apparatus. They introduced in 1800 the first known continuous state nominating convention. Like Republicans in certain other states, they organized each county and township. Committees of correspondence, electioneering committees, and party nominating meetings and conventions were familiar sights around election time. Joint meetings of the legislature made all of the state's appointments, but the Republican lawmakers developed a powerful legislative caucus which almost exclusively controlled the distribution of jobs by the legislature and saw to it that the jobs went to the faithful in the state's thirteen counties. Not only did the caucus distribute state patronage, it also had a voice in dispensing federal posts in the state inasmuch as requests for federal office were often filtered through the caucus. All in all, the caucus was a remarkable example of efficiency in party

organization and the most powerful instrument of party leadership in New Jersey.

The comprehensive nature of Republican patronage apparatus indicates that New Jersey's Jeffersonians had learned early that a political machine draws its strength from zealous party workers and that the workers' zeal was often kindled by possible rewards of office. There were always more applicants than available positions. A prominent New Jersey politican observed late in the Republican era: "Let a vacancy occur, or even be hoped for, in any office or public employment to which even a moderate emolument is awarded—and like the rushing of mighty waters there is a simultaneous press from all quarters toward the aperture." As a result, the Republicans in the legislature maintained a tight rein on available state and federal patronage from 1801 to 1816.

The Republican lawmakers annually dispensed through their caucus 150 or more state jobs according to fixed standards of eligibility and specific allocations by county and region. When passing out jobs each year, they voted in the joint meetings of the legislature virtually as a unit more than 95 per cent of the time. In 1806, which can be taken as an average year, the joint meeting of the legislature made 117 appointments to paying state positions, and 42 militia appointments that carried no stipend. Most of these offices went where the Republican caucus thought they would do the most political good. In addition to such classes of appointments as local judgeships, justices of the peace, county clerkships, state bank positions, militia commissions, and legislature-controlled city posts, there were individual appointments such as secretary of state for New Jersey, state treasurer, clerk of the Assembly, and even the governorship.

Besides these state jobs there was a significant number of federal jobs available in New Jersey. At the beginning of 1802, there were 79 federal appointees in the state. By the end of 1816, the total had risen to 139. Federal places, all remunerative, carried longer terms than the state posts, most of which were for one year. There were fewer federal positions available for frequent redistribution, but because tenure in federal jobs was longer, they were much more desirable. Republicans in New Jersey after 1801 had access to an increasing number of postmasterships. Other openings within the state included customshouse supervisors, collectors, and clerks; internal revenue collectors and assessors; commissioners of loans and bankruptcy; and several lucrative and influential federal court appointments. There was also a superintendent and keeper of the lighthouse at Sandy Hook.

While some positions were pruned from the federal service in New Jersey between 1802 and 1816, notably in the customshouse, the number of postmasters in the state increased sharply. Forty-four of the 79 federal jobs in the state in 1802 came from the Post Office Department; by 1816, postmasterships comprised 114 of the 139 federal positions in New Jersey. Few of these jobs either in the postal service or in other departments of the federal government were very taxing. All permitted the recipient to remain in the state and, if he were so inclined, to carry on his party activities.

How many party workers were appointed to these paying positions, either by the state or federal government? What portion of the total number of officeholders in the state did they represent? What was the relative importance of federal and state patronage in the rewards allocated to party workers? Did the Re-

publicans build and perpetuate a party machine by carefully distributing jobs to the deserving? A survey of active Democratic-Republican workers in the state from 1801 to 1816 discloses some interesting answers to these and other questions about the political use of appointive positions in New Jersey.

For the purposes of the following survey, active party workers are conceived to be those Republicans performing some party function, whose names appear as such, in the Republican newspapers of New Jersey during the period from 1800 through 1816. A further qualification was introduced to avoid sampling those who may have been active for a very brief period: only those whose names appeared at least once a year for two or more years were included. An active party worker is defined as any Democratic-Republican who served for at least two different years on township or county "electioneering" committees, standing committees, or committees of correspondence, who chaired township or county party meetings, or who served as delegates to county or state nominating conventions. The survey does not include Republican candidates for elective office *per se*, although as one would expect many of them fall into the category of "active party worker" in terms of the original definition. The reports of party activities on all levels appearing in the Republican newspapers of New Jersey from 1800 through 1816 reveal the names of 256 men who can be identified as fitting this definition of active party workers.

Three basic areas of patronage are examined here: remunerative state appointive offices, remunerative federal positions, and nonpaying state militia appointments. I have scrutinized each category to discover how many of the 256 identifiable party activists held state or federal jobs during two periods—1801 to 1809 and 1801 through 1816. For the entire interval 1801-16, a meaningful total of 164, or 64.1 per cent, of the 256 party activists were appointed to a paying or honorary post either by the federal or state government. By 1809, 95 or 37.1 per cent of the 256 activists, had already received their jobs.

An analysis of these statistics in terms of state, federal, and militia categories indicates that state appointments, particularly during Jefferson's tenure, comprised the lion's share of offices allotted to Republican activists. During the years 1801-16, of the 256 active workers 139 or 54.3 per cent held paying state offices. Prior to 1809, 85 (33.2 per cent) party men occupied positions carrying stipends distributed by the New Jersey legislature. The federal government through 1816 appointed 29 (11.3 per cent) activists. Far fewer federal appointments were made during Jefferson's Presidency prior to 1809; of the 256 only 5 (2.0 per cent) were elevated to the federal service. Twelve (4.7 per cent) more gained honorary but prestigious state militia commissions through 1816. Of these, 8 (3.1 per cent) were appointed by 1809. *Within these totals*, there were 16 (6.3 per cent) particularly fortunate party men who in the years 1801-16 held both state and federal offices. Up to 1809, only 3 (1.2 per cent) could claim this desirable double bounty for their services to the Republican cause. (All percentage figures given in parentheses are, of course, based on the total of 256 party workers.)

These figures show that, excluding honorary militia posts, 152 individuals who were party activists held paying state or federal jobs—or both—between 1800 and 1817 and that 87 men held these positions between 1800 and 1809. Of the 152, 139 (91.4 per cent) were wholly or partly re-

warded with remunerative state posts. To 1809, the preponderance of activists in state offices is even higher: 85 (97.7 per cent) out of 87. For the years 1801-16, 29 (19.1 per cent) of the 152 Republican officeholders occupied federal office. It is highly significant that this figure was considerably less for the years up to the end of Jefferson's Presidency: only five (5.7 per cent) of 87 officeholders held federal office. (The percentages in each case add up to more than 100 because of the number of men who held both state and federal jobs.) Little of this increase can be attributed either to a growth in the number of federal jobs available during Madison's administration or to a rise in the number of "deserving" workers. The rate of increase in both instances is less than the rate of increase from Jefferson to Madison in the number of party workers receiving federal appointments. If a "spoils system" is a system of rewarding active party workers with paying offices, it appears that, in New Jersey at least, federal appointments became a major factor in contributing to and maintaining such a "system" only during Madison's administrations.

During the years from 1801 through 1816, an estimated 2,000 paying state posts were available for distribution in New Jersey. Nearly all of the positions at the disposal of the legislature were annual appointments. The average number of paying jobs available yearly was taken at 125. (There were 117 paying posts in the state in 1806, not counting the few major state positions with tenure of more than one year. A small but steady increase in the number of places available after 1806 is assumed.) Because the legislators, guided by the caucus, were prone to renew old appointments, an average length of service for an individual in state office may be estimated conservatively at three years. Known Republican activists received 139 paying appointments, which if renewed on an average of twice, totaled approximately 417 paying state appointments in sixteen years. Thus at least 21 per cent of all state offices during the period surveyed probably went to Republican party workers.

The percentage of available federal posts given to active party workers in New Jersey may be fixed more exactly. At the end of 1816, there were 139 federal places in the state; 29 known activists held 31 of these posts. Thus, 22.3 per cent of the total number of federal appointees in New Jersey in late 1816 were known to be active Republican party workers.

Historians have long generalized about the appearance of patronage in the early national period without describing precisely either its specific relation to the state party machines or the extent to which it strengthened party efforts. In New Jersey, the Democratic-Republican interest was not a party of yeoman farmers, but a party of officeholders. Nearly two thirds of the identified Republican activists in the state were rewarded with some appointive public office between 1800 and 1817. There can be no doubt, then, that the Republicans utilized paying offices to create a standing professional cadre of professional party operatives, tangibly dependent upon the success of the party at the polls and therefore willing to give their all for the party. More than 20 per cent of the state and federal appointees were veteran party workers who devoted their personal efforts as well as the weight of their offices to maintaining the party's position. To the activists the party was a source of money, prestige, and power. Thus, the apparatus of the Democratic-Republican party in the township, the county, and the state acquired a degree of depth and permanence it could not otherwise have achieved.

Challenging the view that the franchise was not
democratized until the Jacksonian era, J. R. POLE
(1922-), contends that in Maryland party rivalry greatly
expanded the electorate as competing groups sought
support from new voters previously excluded from the
electoral process. Pole is an English scholar who has
taught and done research in the United States. Reader in
American History and Government and Fellow of
Churchill College at Cambridge University, Pole studied
suffrage reform in Maryland as part of a larger work,
*Political Representation in England and the Origins of
the American Republic* (1966).°

► *Political Parties and
the Right to Vote*

In the post-revolutionary history of the
constitutions of the Atlantic states there is
much that is dramatic, bitter, and even
violent; but there is no transformation
more abrupt and, on the face of it, im-
plausible, than that of Maryland. A man
who had been born in 1776, cradled in
whiggish orthodoxy, would have come of
age in the year when his state extended
the suffrage franchise to all adult white
males without even the requirement of a
tax payment, and would have been able
to bring up his children in a society which
had little to distinguish it from political
democracy. The constitution itself was
subject to amendment by the representatives of the people; the forces, however,
which acted so potently on the constitution were not purely internal. One of
these was the rise of Baltimore, in part a
product of developments in international
trade; the other was the organisation of
national political parties, to which Maryland duly contributed, but by whose
consequences she was in turn deeply
influenced.

In the light of later developments, the
whig concepts which guided the thinking
of the early state constitution-makers
came to look forbiddingly conservative,
and in Maryland more so than in most
other states. Conservative, in an im-

°J. R. Pole, "Constitutional Reform and Election Statistics in Maryland, 1790-1812," *Maryland Historical Magazine*, LV (1960), pp. 275-284. Footnote omitted.

portant sense, they certainly were: they represented, when translated into political institutions, an attempt to build for the future in the form of a prevalent political theory and an equivalent social structure. The general design was that of a political pyramid, comprising a broad base of participation in elections by the common people, and a progressively narrower degree of participation for the ascending scales of elective office. In Maryland, as in most states, the successive levels were marked out by graduated qualifications of property. Under this system, the small group of influential families who had dominated the affairs of the province were able to maintain their grip in the newly-created state.

Even under the proprietory government, whose electoral laws required the ownership of either a fifty-acre freehold or forty pounds personal estate in sterling, there are occasional evidences of participation in elections by a high proportion of the population of free adult males. But the Revolution brought one constitutional reform which, though not startling in form, was to be of irreversible long-term significance. This was the reduction of the personal property qualification for the franchise from forty pounds in sterling (which, of course, was a very hard currency in the late colonial period) to thirty pounds in current money—that is, whatever money was valid under state law; so that the depreciation of wartime currencies must certainly have had the practical effect of extending the suffrage.

A practical extension taking place unintentionally under the aegis of the election law is not the same thing as an extension carried through by legislative intent. There are two sets of evidence on which to base conclusions about the actual state of the suffrage between the making of the constitution of 1776 and its amendment in 1801-02; these are, first the records of disputed elections, and secondly the county-by-county statistics which are now available in serial form from 1790 to 1812. The first question to ask is whether the disappearance of the wartime paper currencies really did have the effect of re-introducing a class of disfranchised Maryland citizens. The fairly frequent practice of challenging election returns by alleging that the result had been won with the aid of unqualified voters makes it clear that such a class had not disappeared in the theory of politics, however elusive it might have been in fact. A disappointed candidate would often throw in this accusation though he may not have expected it to do him much good. What is important, however, is that so long as the challenges were even part of the give and take of hard-fought elections, there must always have been a class for whom the exercise of the suffrage was a matter more of chance than of right. It would be a great mistake to suppose that a high level of suffrage participation under conditions of uncertain legality can be regarded as a satisfactory state of affairs by those who want the franchise as a matter of right. Both Federalists and Republicans, when they began to take organised shape, saw that political capital might be made of the demand, but though the Federalists hesitated, neither did the Republicans at first grasp the opportunity with the quickness or enthusiasm that their advertised principles might have led their admirers to expect.

Long before the advent of political parties, however, the course of Maryland politics had begun to reflect the influences of the overwhelming economic and demographic fact in the state—the growth of Baltimore. No other state was so dominated by the growth of a single town. The population of Baltimore was given as 13,503 in 1790; in 1810, as 46,555; an increase of 244 per cent which should be seen in contrast with a general increase of only 11.4 per cent in the population of the state. By 1798 Baltimore was the nation's third commercial city. The population statistics tell the story not only of Baltimore's rise but of the depopulation or at best, stagnation of many of the southern and East Shore counties. Annapolis, remaining the capital, was reduced to a shadow of its former substance.

Demands for electoral reform in Maryland did not spring in the first place from the issues of party politics. As early as 1791, the House of Delegates passed a bill to abolish all property qualifications for elective office; the bill failed of confirmation in the succeeding session, as required to become a constitutional amendment, but it may be doubted whether the effective leadership in the House would have passed it if they had thought it might lead to a weakening of their position. The constitution provided for voting in the county court of each county, a requirement which caused hardship to those who lived in the remoter villages, especially in the larger, western counties. After some years of dispute, an amendment by which counties were divided into voting districts was passed, in 1800, to remedy this grievance. The measure brought a controversy between the town of Frederick and the country districts but did not follow clearcut party lines although republican principles were stoutly affirmed on both sides. Attempts to suppress cheating and bribery at elections seem to have had little effect.

It was natural that demands for an extension of the suffrage should be made under the existing conditions; and it is also clear that, as the Federalists and Republicans developed beyond the stage of being mere unorganised affinities, into organised and disciplined parties, the Republicans established for themselves a practical connection with the more democratic-looking causes. It may seem uncharitable to suggest that the practical connection preceded that of principle; but the fact is that the issue, when first presented, found the Republicans sharply divided. In 1797 Federalist leaders demonstrated some political acumen by bringing forward the first bill for abolition of all property qualifications for the suffrage, a bill which passed a Federalist House of Delegates to be rejected by a Federalist Senate. A leading part in the opposition was taken by Joseph H. Nicholson, a Republican, whose political standing was so little impaired by this policy that he later became a congressman in his party's interest.

The Federalists came, perhaps, nearer to their true colors when in January, 1799 they attempted to pass an amendment to the constitution to eliminate perjury at elections by requiring the voter to produce documentary evidence of tax assessments to indicate his "worth" at £30 or that he possessed a freehold of fifty acres of land. The enforcement of this measure would certainly have eliminated voters of marginal property. This gave the Republicans their opportunity and thenceforward they took the lead in advocating not only suffrage extension but the secret ballot. Federalists in the House tried to turn the Republican flank by reporting a new bill to do away with property qualifications for the suffrage, which passed by a large majority, only to be turned down once more by the Senate. Since oaths of tax assessment were notoriously productive of perjury, it was logical enough either to require written evidence, or to abolish the property qualification which gave rise to the need. It was only after the tax assessment act had been passed that the parties began to treat this issue as a matter of electoral policy; but the incompleteness of party organisation is shown by the Federalist Senate's rejection of the move, by the Federalists in the House, to extend the franchise. To the common voter, it could only mean that the Republicans were the party of constitutional reform, dividing the parties on grounds of constitutional principle, which was just the impression that the House Federalists were evidently trying to avoid.

Divided though they might be on principle, the parties were little different in social substance. Both parties found support in slave-owning and plantation-controlled areas; smaller farming interests were more inclined to go Republican. The towns moved steadily towards the Republicans, who seem to have been able to enlist the mechanics and artisans; by 1803 only Georgetown remained Federalist. The leadership of both parties was provided by those who had traditionally governed: planters, merchants and lawyers. It was the familiar convention of the period, a government of the gentry, consolidated, not undermined, by a broadening basis of popular participation.

When the Republicans came into power in Maryland they demonstrated both the extent and the limits of their reformist intentions. They gained control of the House of Delegates in 1800, after a campaign in which interest was concentrated on the issue of legislative as opposed to popular choice of presidential electors. The Federalists had proposed to vest the choice of electors in the state legislature, a reversal of existing procedure, in order to offset the general ticket system which the Jeffersonians, equally for party purposes, had introduced in Virginia. The Federalist defeat in the House elections was followed in

1801 by Republican success in the quinquennial elections for the Senate. With control of the legislature at last established, they carried out their programme by passing the act which extended the suffrage to all adult white males and by re-passing it, to effect a constitutional amendment, in the next session. It was in this act that the word "white" was first added to the list of the qualifications of voters, a significant feature of that expansion of general interest in politics which culminated—or—recurred—in the Jacksonian period. It was in the constitutional revisions of (loosely speaking) the Jacksonian period that the exclusion of free Negroes from political life was completed in the South, and their restriction carried further in the North. The ballot was introduced in 1803 as part of the same measure.

Popular interest and participation in elections ran very high in many states in the Jeffersonian period. Party organisation reached into counties and townships and was supported by a vigorous and frequently partisan press. All this is not to be attributed to an adventitious or artificially stimulated excitement: the issues of the period were intrinsically important and go far to explain the rise of party politics. The parties, in turn, developed an interest in the issues that would maintain them in power or restore them to it. The statistics show a marked rise in the level of participation by voters from 1796 to 1800; and a distinct overall increase again in the congressional elections of 1803. It seems likely that the abolition of suffrage qualifications brought more men into the elections of that year; but a close examination shows that there had been outbursts of electoral activity which, in the majority of counties, had produced equally high figures in years before suffrage reform. In five counties, Allegheny, Calvert, Frederick, Harford and Washington, the voting in 1803 was outstandingly higher than ever before; in the remaining fourteen, there were occasional precedents for equally high voting. Suffrage restrictions may not have been working either uniformly or effectively, but their removal went far towards satisfying popular aspirations for political equality and left the parties more freedom to develop their electoral strategy. The elimination of the harrassing uncertainty as to the right to vote must be counted a positive gain both for individual voter and for political organiser.

It would be a mistake, however, to see the parties of this formative period in a modern light, outlined by modern definitions. There are marked signs that the Senate, even under Republican control, still stood for the social principles which had inspired its foundation. It was by its constitution more remote than the House from the direct influence of the people, and it interpreted the maintenance of that remoteness as one of its constitutional duties. When, in 1804, the House passed a bill providing for the direct election of the Senate by the people, the upper chamber defended itself by adding a totally unacceptable amendment for proportional representation in the lower house. The senate also defended the special position of the governor, rejecting, in January, 1805, a House bill for popular election. It may be added that many Republicans in the House had failed to support this bill.

International affairs, and Jeffersonian foreign policy, would not permit political issues to subside. Both parties seem, after 1808, to have realised that future strength would be drawn from enlisting popular support throughout the constitutional process rather than by the maintenance of graduated restrictions. By the next wave

of reforms, coming in 1809, all property qualifications were removed from appointive and elective office. Religious equality was also put on a constitutional basis. But the indirect system of election of governor, council and Senate was left untouched. Popular election of presidential electors and representatives in Congress was made part of the constitution at the same time. Direct election of senators in the counties was introduced in 1837. The Council was then abolished and the governorship was opened to popular election.

While the constitution of Maryland had been growing more democratic, there was one important respect in which its effects, by mere conservatism, had been growing steadily more undemocratic. This was the basis of representation in the House of Delegates, unchanged throughout this period and left intact by the reforms of 1809-1810. Each county was entitled to four, Baltimore and Annapolis each to two, members in the lower house. With the attrition of population in the lower counties, the vast growth of Baltimore, and the thickening of settlement in western counties, this system developed, without attention, the characteristics of an ingrown gerrymander. The agrarian interests, watching the rise of the city with distrust, clung to a system which afforded them a form of defence against the representation of numbers. It could be seen, philosophically, as a continuation of the respectable whig concept of a government devised to incorporate and protect a variety of economic and professional interests; but in blunt fact it was a safeguard against the rule of the majority.

Intimations of the strength of this majority had been given as early as 1790, in which year the reader's scepticism is likely to be aroused by the extraordinary turnout of the voters of Baltimore. The returns show a poll by adult males that barely halts itself at 100 per cent. The explanation lies in an intense struggle for control of the state's congressional delegation between the interests centered on the Chesapeake and those on the Potomac. The Baltimore vote was the decisive factor in the Chesapeake victory.

In such conditions, there could not be much permanent hope of controlling the political process by constitutional restraints on the suffrage. Popularity could too easily be whipped up by candidates making claims on behalf of those who were disfranchised, or whose position was doubtful. The future lay with those who could mobilise the franchise of the masses, not with those who would restrict it. This, in retrospect, is plain enough; and a certain interest must attach to the problem of explaining the apparent reticence of the Jeffersonians of Maryland in setting about this task of mobilisation. Some of their leaders, in both House and Senate, seem to have thought that the tasks of a Republican party of opposition to Federalist policies could be discharged by the recognized social and political leaders, under existing constitutional safeguards; it was only after hesitation, as constitutional reform became linked with party politics, that the Republicans agreed in proclaiming the connection between their general principles and the specific demands for a greater measure of popular participation in the political life of the state. If the problems of that political life are considered within the context of the deeply ingrained sense of social order and the habits of deference which characterised the eighteenth century and

were formally expressed by the constitution of 1776, and if the continuity of the Republican leadership with that social order is also understood, then it may be suggested that the impetus to Republican organisation was not in its origin an impetus to constitutional reform. Reform came quickly, and was taken up in fact by both parties; but it was a consequence rather than a cause of their formation.

Before political parties, the social conditions of reform were brought into existence by the rise of Baltimore. This, in Maryland, is the outstanding feature of the period; but its implications reach far beyond the bounds of the state, and make of Maryland herself an astonishing forcing-house of the democratic process, against all expectation, and against the intentions of the framers of her recent constitution. The whig principles embodied in the constitution were essentially similar to those of Virginia, though they were actually applied in Maryland with more care and elaboration. In both states, these institutions eventually crumbled before the great equalizing forces that were to take command in the nineteenth century. These forces did not rise from any single source. But it is surely one of the most striking facts about the history of these developments that the complex and carefully guarded constitutional structure of Maryland gave way before the democracy of the great sea-port city of Baltimore a full generation earlier than the defences of the old order in Virginia were reduced by forces which sprang from the settlement of the West.

In the early years of the Republic, banks were not merely financial institutions but corporations deeply invested with political significance. BRAY HAMMOND (1886-   ), a leading student of the relationship between banks and politics, had a long career in banking that included twenty years of service at the Federal Reserve Board (1930-1950). Winner of a Pulitzer Prize in History, Hammond challenged the Beardian school of historians who regard the Bank of the United States as an instrument by which conservative capitalist groups advanced their interests at the expense of the majority. According to Beard, the Republican party, which championed the interests of the agrarian masses, was suspicious of banks in general and hostile to the national bank in particular. Hammond argues that the Republicans included entrepreneurial elements who wanted to share in the profits of banking and who used political influence to widen opportunities for those excluded from Federalist-dominated enterprises.°

► Parties and the Democratization of Business Enterprise

Its silence about banks notwithstanding, the Constitution became involved in the subject in its second year, when Alexander Hamilton in December 1790, during the third session of the first Congress, submitted his plan for a National Bank. The plan was embodied in the second of the several great reports prepared by him during the early years of his secretaryship of the Treasury, the others being on manufactures and on public credit. In these reports he outlined the major elements of a program for raising up a powerful and prosperous nation. The factors already given were immense material resources—utilized chiefly so far in agriculture and in maritime shipping—an energetic, multiplying population, and the private credit of individual men of wealth. The factors needed were manufactures and public credit. Hamilton's program combined magnitude and comprehensiveness, on the one hand, with, on the other, meticulousness in detail and a thorough understanding of all he was talking about. The reasonable convictions he had had in 1779 respecting the utility of a bank had been confirmed by the experience of the three banks that had been established since. He now wished to have one set up that should directly and adequately serve

° Reprinted from *Banks and Politics in America, from the Revolution to the Civil War* by Bray Hammond by permission of Princeton University Press. Copyright © 1957 by Princeton University Press. Pages 114-122, 145-164. Footnotes omitted.

the needs of the federal government, which was to incorporate it and own a substantial share of its capital.

The proposed institution was not simply another commercial bank. Like the Bank of England, it would conduct commercial business but would also do far more. It would be an important aid to the new federal government in collecting taxes and in administering the public finances; it would be a source of loans to the Treasury. Subscriptions to its capital might be paid one-fourth in gold and silver coin and three fourths in obligations of the federal government. This arrangement would provide sufficient capital to support an extensive circulation, but it would also enhance the current price of government obligations and thereby sustain the government's credit. . . .

Opponents of the proposal objected that the Constitution conveyed no authority to form a bank of any other kind of corporation and that by chartering one the federal government would be disregarding the limitations of its powers and interfering with the rights of the states. James Madison, now a member of the House of Representatives, pointed out that the proposed institution "would interfere so as indirectly to defeat a state bank at the same place," and would "directly interfere with the rights of states to prohibit as well as to establish banks." The proposal for a national bank, he said, "was condemned by the silence of the Constitution; was condemned by the rule of interpretation arising out of the Constitution; was condemned by its tendency to destroy the main characteristic of the Constitution; was condemned by the expositions of the friends of the Constitution whilst depending before the public; was condemned by the apparent intentions of the parties which ratified the Constitution; was condemned by the ex-

planatory amendments proposed by Congress themselves to the Constitution; and he hoped it would receive its final condemnation by the vote of this House." For more than a bank was at stake; the constructions of the Constitution that had been maintained in the course of the arguments for it, Madison said, went "to the subversion of every power whatever in the several states."

Secretary Hamilton's proposal was also subjected to an agrarian attack like that the Bank of North America had sustained in the Pennsylvania Assembly five years before. Banks, it was averred, were a corrupting influence and would destroy the free institutions of the New World. "What was it drove our forefathers to this country?" demanded an agrarian representative from Georgia, James Jackson. "Was it not the ecclesiastical corporations and perpetual monopolies of England and Scotland? Shall we suffer the same evils to exist in this country, instead of taking every possible method to encourage the increase of emigrants to settle among us? For, if we establish the precedent now before us, there is no saying where it shall stop." He said the bank was "calculated to benefit a small part of the United States—the mercantile interest only; the farmers, the yeomanry of the country, will derive no advantage from it." William B. Giles of Virginia presumed "that a law to punish with death those who counterfeit the paper emitted by the bank, will be consequent upon the existence of this act; hence a judicial decision will probably be had of the most serious and awful nature. The life of an individual at stake on one hand; an improvident act of the government on the other." Eventually at least one man was put to death for counterfeiting notes of the Bank; and this fact was urged twenty years later by another Virginian, Senator Brent, as one of the things that made the bank constitutional by practice and acquiescence. . . .

Mr Jefferson, grudging even that the Bank might be a convenience, was positive that it was not a necessity. And, he asked, "Can it be thought that the Constitution intended that, for a shade or two of convenience, more or less, Congress should be authorized to break down the most ancient and fundamental laws of the several states, such as those against mortmain, the laws of alienage, the rules of descent, the acts of distribution, the laws of escheat and forfeiture, the laws of monopoly? Nothing but a necessity invincible by any other means can justify such a prostration of laws which constitute the pillars of our whole system of jurisprudence." Mr Jefferson could not abide considerations of administrative advantage which seemed to him to put an efficient working of the governmental machinery before the maintenance of a simple society composed as wholly as possible of individual human beings and as little as possible of institutions.

Hamilton on his part could not abide what seemed to him Thomas Jefferson's visionary and anarchic metaphysics, which he believed "would be fatal to the just and indispensable authority of the United States." He declared that it was the purpose of the Constitution to set up a workable government and that to find it frustrating that purpose at the very outset was preposterous. He countered with a sweeping and audacious assertion of federal sovereignty: "Now, it appears to the Secretary of the Treasury that this general principle is inherent in the very definition of government and essential to every step of the progress to be made by that of the United States; namely, that every power vested in a government is in its nature *sovereign* and includes, by force of the term, a right to employ all the means req-

uisite and fairly applicable to the attainment of the ends of such power and which are not precluded by restrictions and exceptions specified in the constitution, or not immoral, or not contrary to the essential ends of political society." These words, which proved to have a potency for far more than establishment of the Bank, evidently satisfied the President; he did not use the veto he had asked Mr Madison to prepare but signed the act incorporating the Bank, 25 February 1791.

It is obvious that in the beginning the political prominence of banking in the United States outstripped its economic importance. When there were still only three banks in the country, the subject engaged an inordinate amount of attention. The proposed National Bank became so much a political and constitutional issue that far more was said of it as such than is of record respecting its operation and economic significance. . . .

The people who were most eager for a strong central government and who wished to apply the Constitution constructively were the people who also wanted banks. They were the commercial and monied class. They were men of substance, they were creditors of the government, and they had a natural wish to recover what they had risked on American independence. This wish was identical with the wish that there be a strong and effective government to maintain that independence.

Their opponents were principally agrarians who had been mistrustful of the Constitution and were now mistrustful of the central government created by it. They were mistrustful of all business interests. Those in the Pennsylvania Assembly who in 1785 had almost annihilated the Bank of North America attempted two years later to keep Pennsylvania from ratifying the Constitution; and in Congress the same group maintained a consistent hostility not only to the Bank of the United States but to other Hamiltonian measures. They, too, like the merchants had wanted political independence, but to them independence and a strong central government were incompatible. They saw in the latter the replacement of the British yoke with a Hamiltonian one.

Hamilton's proposal of a federal Bank was a plain defiance of agrarian interests and of the view that the powers of the federal government were definitely limited. In their reception of it, Madison in Congress and Jefferson in his report to Washington both affirmed what shortly became embodied in the tenth amendment—that in effect the federal government possessed only the powers given it. Jefferson said that he considered "the foundation of the Constitution as laid on this ground." The ideas later developed and enunciated in the Kentucky and Virginia Resolutions of 1798, where the Constitution was asserted to be a compact between sovereign states and the general government to be one with special purpose and possessed of delegated, limited powers only, were already clearly present in Jefferson's and Madison's arguments against the Bank in 1791. On the other hand, it was in defense of his proposal for a federal Bank that Hamilton made to President Washington the statement of federal sovereignty I have quoted—a statement that has governed constitutional jurisprudence ever since. . . .

Alexander Hamilton prepared America for an imperial future of wealth and power, mechanized beyond the handicraft stage of his day, and amply provided with credit to that end. Thomas Jefferson represented the yeomanry and designed for America a future of competence and simplicity, agrarian, and without the enticing subtleties of credit. Writing in Paris in 1785 to a correspondent in the Netherlands, he said that were he to indulge his own theory, he would wish the United States "to practice neither commerce nor navigation but to stand, with respect to Europe, precisely on the footing of China." All American citizens should be farmers, selling their surplus produce to those nations that should come to seek it. But this he acknowledged was theory only; Americans had a decided taste for navigation and commerce, which they took from their mother country, and their government was in duty bound to calculate all its measures accordingly. Yet in another letter, written at Monticello to John Adams in 1812, he said with satisfaction that in his part of the country every family was a manufactory within itself, producing with its own materials and labor all the stouter and middling stuffs for its own clothing and household use. "We consider a sheep for every person in the family as sufficient to clothe it, in addition to the cotton, hemp, and flax which we raise ourselves." And in a surge of the sanguine idealism he had professed to give up thirty years before, he went on: "The economy and thriftiness resulting from our household manufactures are such that they will never again be laid aside, and nothing more salutary for us has ever happened than the British obstructions to our demands for their manufactures." Now, it is clear that a man who at every opportunity turned passionately to the agrarian ideal, seeing in the agrarian way of life an advantageousness, a purity, and a humanity with which commerce and industrialization were incompatible, should hate banks. For banking presupposed a complex, specialized economy which found a flexible monetary supply indispensable and the notion of a sheep for every member of the family, to provide its stouter and middling stuffs, something to laugh at. Americans still maintain a pharisaical reverence for Thomas Jefferson, but they have in reality little use for what he said and believed—save when, on occasion and out of context, it appears to be of political expediency. What they really admire is what Alexander Hamilton stood for, and his are the hopes they have fulfilled. . . .

In 1791, when the Bank of the United States was chartered, the Federalists, a monied minority of the population, were in control of the government, and there were three banks in operation. In 1811, when the Bank of the United States was let die, the Federalists were disintegrated, the Jeffersonians had long been in power, and banks, which were one of that party's principal traditionary aversions, had multiplied from three to ninety. In the next five years the number increased to nearly 250; by 1820 it exceeded 300—an increase of more than a hundred-fold in the first thirty years of the federal union. It is hard to imagine how banking could have been propagated more under its sponsors than it was under its "enemies."

That banking flourished with the decline of Hamilton's party and the ascendancy of Jefferson's connotes the fact that business was becoming democratic. It was no longer a select and innumerous aristocracy—business opportunities were falling open to everyone. The result was an alignment of the new generation of business men with the genuine agrarians, whose rugged individualism constituted the Jeffersonian democracy's professed faith and required very little alteration to fit enterprise as well. The success of the Republican party in retaining the loyalty of the older agrarians while it recruited among the newer entrepreneurial masses

was possible, Professor Beard has explained, because Jefferson's academic views pleased the one group and his practical politics propitiated the other. It was also because equality of opportunity in business and the principle of *laisser faire* could be advocated with a Jeffersonian vocabulary.

The number of banks grew from 6 to 246 in the twenty-five years between establishment of the Bank of the United States in 1791 and establishment of a new Bank of the United States in 1816. This growth was not the multiplication of something familiar, like houses or ships or carriages, but a multiplication of something unfamiliar or even mysterious. Had banks been thought to be merely depositories where savings were tucked away—as came to be thought in time— there would have been nothing remarkable about their increase. But they were known to do more than receive money. They were known to create it. For each dollar paid in by the stockholders, the banks lent two, three, four, or five. The more sanguine part of the people were happy to have it so, no matter if they did not understand how it could be. The more conservative, like John Adams, thought it a cheat. Since the Republican party had both its agrarian wing and its speculative-entrepreneurial wing, it came to include both the conspicuous opponents of banking and the conspicuous advocates of it.

The Jeffersonian impetus in banking may well have begun in reaction to the Federalist character of the first banks, all of which were conceived and defended as monopolies. The surest procedure for any new group that wished to obtain a bank charter from a Jeffersonian state legislature was to cry out against monopoly in general and in particular against that of the Federalist bankers who would lend nothing, it was alleged, to good Republicans. The argument was persuasive. Jeffersonians, if they could not extirpate monopoly, could at least reduce its inequities by seizing a share of its rewards. So Jefferson himself seems to have thought. "I am decidedly in favor of making all the banks Republican," he wrote Gallatin in July 1803, "by sharing deposits among them in proportion to the dispositions they show." Dr Benjamin Rush wrote to John Adams in 1810 that though Federalist and Democratic principles were ostensibly at issue between the parties, "the true objects of strife are a 'mercantile bank' by the former and a 'mechanics bank' by the latter party." The State Bank of Boston solicited federal deposits in 1812, following the demise of the Bank of the United States, with the assurance to the Republican administration that the State Bank was "the property of sixteen hundred freemen of the respectable state of Massachusetts, all of them advocates of the then existing federal administration, associated not solely for the purpose of advancing their pecuniary interests but for the more noble purpose of cherishing Republican men and Republican measures against the wiles and machinations" of the rival political party. The same course could be followed by any sort of special interest— geographic, economic, or what not— which wanted credit and was dissatisfied with the existing banks. So the number grew. Each borrowing interest wanted a bank of its own. Soon, as Dr Rush said, banks were serving not only merchants but "mechanics," on whose skills the Industrial Revolution was progressing, and farmers. The charter of the Washington Bank, Westerly, Rhode Island, June 1800, solicited both interests. It recited that "added to those common arguments in favour of bank institutions, such as pro-

moting punctuality in discharge of contracts, . . .and extending commerce by accumulating the means of carrying it on, there are also arguments in favour of such establishments, as promoting the agricultural and mechanical interest of our country." It declared that "those banks which at present are established in this state are too remote or too confined in their operations to diffuse their benefits so generally to the country as could be wished." It mentioned the embarrassments into which "the farmer is frequently drove for the want of means of stocking his farm at those seasons of the year when money is obtained with the greatest difficulty"; and it expressed the belief that "in a place peculiarly fitted by nature to encourage the industry and ingenuity of the mechanic by holding out the sure prospects of a profitable return for his enterprise, nothing is wanting but those little assistances from time to time which banks only can give."

The next step beyond making banks ancillary to agriculture and industry was to make them ancillary to public improvements of large scale. In 1809 it was proposed in Congress that the Bank of the United States be replaced by "a general national establishment of banks throughout the United States" whose profits should be devoted to public roads, canals, and schools. In the individual states such proposals were put into effect. Sometimes banking was the real object of the incorporators, and the enterprise or "public improvement" was merely a blind or an excuse; sometimes banking was really subordinate, or at any rate not the sole object.

In 1791 American business had been concerned mainly with foreign commerce; by 1816 it was concerned mainly with a greatly diversified internal economy. The change had been impelled chiefly by the abundance of native resources to be developed, but it was hastened and intensified by the Napoleonic wars, which for two decades or so kept Britain and France at one another's throats and involved all Europe besides, driving Britain to strike at France s trade with the United States and France to strike at Britain's. American seaborne commerce was battered from both sides. War with either or both belligerents overhung the country for years and broke out at last, with Britain, in 1812. It ended in 1814. By then the dominant interests of American business had been turned decisively toward the domestic field; and the potential demand for bank credit had been enlarged both in volume and in variety.

Before the turn of the century, politics had been roiled by the Jay Treaty, the X Y Z affair, the Alien and Sedition Acts, and the Kentucky and Virginia Resolutions. After the turn of the century, the Embargo of 1807, the Non-Intercourse Act of 1809, and war in 1812 made matters still worse. Disunion itself came within speaking distance. There was extreme economic and social instability: expansion, migration, and realignment of interests. The population, which in 1790 had been 3,900,000, became 9,600,000 by 1810; and by 1812 the original thirteen states had become eighteen. Through migration and settlement all the territory east of the Mississippi had become American—save Florida, which was shortly, in 1819, to be picked up—and in the Louisiana Purchase, 1803, half the territory beyond the Mississippi had been acquired. In 1793 the cotton gin had been invented and the way cleared for Cotton to become King and the leading means of payment for the goods required from Europe for the building up of American industry. The steamship *Clermont* made her pristine passage up and down the Hudson in 1807. By 1810, manufacturing with water power had suddenly become common; the number of cotton mills in 1807 was fifteen and of spindles 8,000, but in 1811 those numbers had grown to eighty-seven and 80,000. These and other profound changes that were going on with violent rapidity and literally changing the face of the earth with roads, canals, factories, and cities, did not yet shake agriculture from its basic place in the economy; they did, however, raise up mechanical industry and inland transportation to rival and in time surpass foreign commerce, which had originally shared with agriculture the country's economic activity.

It is obvious that this immense expansion of business could not be the work of an established, limited group of capitalists. It was the work of immigrants and of native Americans born on farms—self-made men with energy, ingenuity, and an outstanding need of money with which to finance their enterprises. Most of them did not become millionaires, but they were business men, nevertheless.

The relative importance of New York and Philadelphia was becoming very different at the end of the 18th century from what it had been a half-century before. Benjamin Franklin had been drawn to Philadelphia; Alexander Hamilton and Aaron Burr had since been drawn to New York. Philadelphia was a city of great wealth, but New York was a city of enterprise. A newer and more aggressive spirit, in both politics and business, flourished there, and though Philadelphia was to remain till about 1840 the financial center of America, one can see by 1800 not only the natural advantages New York possessed, but a characteristic energy and ingenuity that seem to explain her triumphant exploitation of them.

In New York City, from 1784 to 1791 there was no bank but the Bank of New York, and from 1791 to 1799 there was no other but the local office of the Bank of the United States. Both were Federalist. During those fifteen years, though business growth was substantial, the establishment of other banks was obstructed partly by Federalist protection of the two banks already established and partly by conservative opposition, largely agrarian, to banking in general. But in 1799, through a skilful stratagem of Aaron Burr's, a corporate charter was obtained under which a new bank was set up, the Bank of the Manhattan Company, of far greater size than the Bank of New York, of much wider proprietorship, and Jeffersonian in its political ties. Its establishment was an important event in both economic and political history.

Colonel Burr was provided an opportunity for his stratagem by the pestilence of yellow fever in New York the previous summer. A joint committee of the Common Council and other local bodies reported the following winter that amongst "the means of removing the causes of pestilential diseases" it considered "a plentiful supply of fresh water as one of the most powerful," and it earnestly recommended "that some plan for its introduction into this city be carried into execution as soon as possible." New York was then dependent upon ponds, wells, cisterns, and the carting of water in from the country for sale. In accordance with the joint committee's report, bills authorizing various hygienic measures and in particular the construction of water works by the city were introduced in the legislature at Albany. They failed to receive attention. Late in February 1799, Mayor Varick of New York City informed the Common Council of a visit he had just received from a group of six gen-

tlemen, prominent residents of the city, who were concerned about the status of the bills. They were Aaron Burr, one of the city's Republican representatives in the state legislature, which was still Federalist; Alexander Hamilton, now engaged in private legal practice; John Murray, a wealthy Quaker merchant, then president of the Chamber of Commerce and formerly a director of the Bank of New York; Gulian Verplanck, Federalist, president of the Bank of New York; Peter Wendover, Republican, president of the Mechanics Society; and John Broome, Republican, formerly president of the Chamber of Commerce. Their concern as reported by Colonel Burr was lest the legislators reject the proposed bills, there being discontent with the plan to enlarge the Council's powers, even to protect the city's health. He thought it "problematical whether those bills would pass in the form proposed" and suggested that the Council request the legislature, if the bills were not deemed proper in the form proposed, to "make such provisions on the several subjects thereof as to them should appear most eligible." Fresh proposals to this end were then suggested by Alexander Hamilton. These were that the Council, instead of seeking authority to build and operate the water works itself, favor incorporating a business company for the purpose. . . .

The Council responded wholeheartedly. The legislature was apprised by resolution of what had occurred and of the Council's realization that by the terms of the bills then pending its cares and duties would be considerably extended and its members "subjected to great additional trouble without any emolument to themselves." The council also mentioned the possibility "that a company would be best adapted to the business of supplying the city with water"; although in public and official opinion till then city ownership of the water works had been preferred to private. It emphasized its anxiety that measures for the water supply and the city's health be authorized, disclaimed any attachment to the pending bills, and assured the legislature of its acquiescence in whatever the legislators should decide was best. . . .

The bill designated the corporation the "President and Directors of the Manhattan Company" and authorized a capital of $2,000,000, which was twice what Mr Hamilton had mentioned, and the city was to own a tenth and not a third. The bill also designated the first directors; the majority, including Mr Burr, were Republicans, but Federalists had some prominence of place. Further, after giving the corporation the necessary power to erect dams, divert streams, lay pipes, etc., etc., the bill provided in Section 8 "That it shall and may be lawful for the said company to employ all such surplus capital as may belong or accrue to the said company in the purchase of public or other stock or in any other monied transactions or operations not inconsistent with the constitution and laws of this state or of the United States, for the sole benefit of the said company."

The bill passed the lower house apparently without question. Since there were Federalists outside the legislature willing to put money in the project, it is not strange that there were Federalists inside willing to vote for it. But in a committee of the upper house one senator wished to have the plenary clause I have just quoted stricken out. "Mr Burr," according to Matthew L. Davis, his friend and biographer, "promptly and frankly informed the honourable member that it not only did authorize but that it was intended the directors should use the surplus capital in any way they thought

expedient and proper. That they might have a bank, an East India Company, or anything else that they deemed profitable. That the mere supplying the city with water would not of itself remunerate the stockholders. Colonel Burr added that the senator was at liberty to communicate this explanation to other members and that he had no secrecy on the subject." Because of this explanation, probably, and not in spite of it, the bill was passed. Its real object, according to the conservatives, was "to furnish new projects and means for speculation." . . .

The measure became law, 2 April 1799. Less than a fortnight latter the company began negotiations with the Council about the water supply.

It also got under way with its plans for a bank. Robert Troup, a conservative and Federalist, reported to his friend Rufus King, 19 April 1799: "It is given out that we are to have a new bank established by the Company and that they will also embark deeply in the East India Trade and perhaps turn their attention to marine insurance." He said that "The most respectable mercantile and monied interests are opposed to the measure; and they attach much blame as well to the Council of Revision as to the Assembly and Senate. I have no doubt that if the company carry their schemes into effect, they will contribute powerfully to increase the bloated state of credit which has of late essentially injured us by repeated and heavy bankruptcies." A few weeks later, 5 June, he mentions "a resolution of the Manhattan Company lately announced to set up a new bank." Less than a year later the Manhattan advertised its readiness to insure lives and arrange annuities. Its main interest, however, was its banking business, which its aggressive management and close association with the rising Jeffersonian or Republican party developed rapidly into the largest in the city and the state. . . .

Alexander Hamilton, Gulian Verplanck, and John Murray would not knowingly have helped Aaron Burr to get a banking charter more valuable than the Bank of New York's. But that they would help one of the city's legislative representatives in a business-like effort to get the city a fit water supply was to be expected. They were public-spirited, normally susceptible to flattery, and doubtless glad to join magnanimously with political opponents for the city's good and the furtherance of enterprise. Aaron Burr knew how to value, to obtain, and to use their assistance. No better means of obscuring and furthering his purpose can be thought of than his having with him at the start three men so closely associated with the banks to which his own would be a powerful rival. . . .

Aaron Burr's ruse was more than just a trick. It was a minor revolution, economic and political. It illustrates the larger revolution which in the country as a whole was changing the disciplined and restricted economy of the 18th century into the dynamic, complex, *laisser faire* economy of the 19th century. It illustrates the repressive hold that the Federalists, who ten years before had established the central government, were trying to maintain on business and that was driving the party's less patient adherents into the rebellious Republican fold. For the city of New York to have gone on much longer with only the Bank of New York and the office of the Bank of the United States was out of the question. The energy and ambition of its business community were too great. The Federalists had brilliantly advanced business enterprise but could not long dominate it. The party was to linger on, monied and ineffective, while its young men flocked incongruously into Mr Jefferson's Republican ranks and later into General Andrew Jackson's Democratic ones; where they made it part of the destiny of those two popular leaders and enemies of privilege to clear the way for a new, larger, and more powerful class of money-makers than could have existed before enterprise became democratic.

According to Matthew L. Davis, Colonel Burr was "lauded by the Democratic party for his address and they rejoiced in his success." For now they too had a bank and a bigger one than the Federalists. . . .

Indeed, the prevailing view of New York Republicans was the following, expressed by James Cheetham in 1804: "It is well known that previous to the incorporation of the Manhattan Company, the Branch Bank and the New York Bank, governed by *federal* gentlemen, were employed in a great measure as *political engines*. A close system of exclusion against those who differed from them on political subjects was adopted and pursued. There were but few active and useful Republicans that could obtain from those banks discount accommodations. . . . The incorporation of the Manhattan Company corrected the evil. All parties are now accommodated."

A party divided against itself cannot survive. Federalists learned this lesson during their years of defeat and disintegration as a national political force after 1800. In the following selection, STEPHEN G. KURTZ (1926-   ), of the Institute of Early American History, examines the closing years of Federalist supremacy in the late 1790s to discover the sources of division within the party. Assuming that disunity was responsible for Federalist decline, historians must explain why the split in the Federalist party went so deep and why the urgencies of being the minority party out of power did not bring warring factions together. According to Kurtz, President John Adams' decision to avoid war with France was good for the country but seriously undermined his party's future and his own chances for re-election.°

The Split in the Federalist Party

Three months after his inauguration John Adams called Congress together and in a solemn address recommended that measures for defense be immediately taken. Among the specific measures requested was that for a provisional army. He asked that officers be commissioned and arrangements for recruiting worked out, though he did not call for the establishment of a large professional army. Throughout the two years during which the possibility of war hung perilously close Adams made it clear that he put his faith in a strong navy and cared little for an army as an instrument of either defense or foreign policy. All he asked was

that plans be made. His responsibility as President demanded that he take such a line so long as he believed war a possibility, and he was convinced that France could only be brought around to treat with American envoys on an even basis if it were made clear that Americans were prepared to fight rather than submit to further humiliation.

Federalists in Congress, both Adams men and Hamiltonians, far overstepped the arms limits laid down by the President, however. In 1799 Hamilton, as Inspector General and virtual commander of the army, attempted to recruit the twenty-thousand-man force allowed for

°Reprinted from *The Adams Presidency* by Stephen G. Kurtz by permission of the University of Pennsylvania Press. Copyright © 1957 by the University of Pennsylvania Press. Pages 307-333. Footnotes omitted.

by the laws of the Fifth Congress, and more than enough officers were commissioned to command the additional thirty thousand provisional troops that would be brought into service when and if the President saw fit to announce a full wartime emergency. Federalist leaders were convinced that an army was necessary, some because they considered war a likelihood and others because they anticipated a Southern rebellion. Hamilton and his intimate friends had private reasons for throwing themselves energetically into the work of creating a national army.

The Alien and Sedition Acts have so overshadowed the history of John Adams' administration that the vast significance of the army has been uniformly underestimated. The threat to freedom of speech contained in the Alien and Sedition Acts roused Jefferson and his friends to new enthusiasm for battle, but if the political history of Adams' administration is viewed from the Federalist point of view—from the viewpoint of the collapse of the Federalists rather than the rise of the Jeffersonians—the army reveals itself as the most significant single issue of that violent four-year period.

"The army," wrote John Quincy Adams, "was the first decisive symptom of a schism in the Federal party itself, which accomplished its final overthrow and that of the administration." When Adams broke the war crisis in February, 1799, by reopening negotiations with France, he put an abrupt end to the plans of the vindictive, militaristic faction that had seized control of the Federalist party. Adams believed that his action would be widely applauded and there is strong evidence to show that his chances for reelection were enhanced by the inauguration of the second peace mission rather than ruined by it, as Hamiltonians insisted. He gambled on the hope that the Hamiltonian wing of the party would be forced to follow his lead and accept a decision that circumstances made both necessary and expedient.

High-ranking Federalists welcomed the war crisis whether they believed it a bluff on the part of France or the prelude to actual hostilities. They had crept back into power in 1796 by too narrow a margin not to have seized upon the sudden discomfiture of the Republicans without delight. The fencesitters in Congress had swung over completely, and the public showed unmistakable signs of approving the administration's policy. A few powerful leaders wished to let no chance slip of destroying the opposition. . . .

The most forthright and selfish demands for war came from New England Federalists. Stephen Higginson, who had just been appointed a government naval agent, placed the highest premium upon political survival. "Nothing but an open war can save us," he wrote to Oliver Wolcott, Jr.,[1] in July, "and the more inveterate and deadly it shall be, the better will be our chance for security in the future." The blood of the nation was worth spilling for the sake of sound politics and possible fortunes, though undoubtedly Higginson considered himself a true patriot and a champion of sound political principles. . . .

Republican fears that their opponents desired war were not fabricated for electioneering purposes, nor were the worst suspicions as to the motives behind that desire unfounded. War would deal a death blow to Jefferson and his friends far more effectively than the most strenuously waged campaign for votes, and with surprising frankness Federalist leaders

[1] Oliver Wolcott, Jr., Secretary of the Treasury under Adams.—Ed.

admittedly sought to deliver such a blow. Many sincerely believed that France had already begun to wage war without formally announcing it, and the desire to strike back was understandable. The editor of a small town New England newspaper, for example, printed a long list of French attacks upon American naval vessels for the winter of 1798 and then asked, "If the United States are not now in a state of war with France; in what state are they? Let the Loganites answer the question."

As happens often in politics, men in high places acted during the war scare on the basis of their fears and not upon well-established facts. Many Federalists in 1798 were convinced that rebellion was about to commence in the South and in the western frontier areas of the nation close to Spanish colonial outposts. . . .

When the Federalists called for a standing army and began to raise one it was assumed that the talk of a French invasion was nothing more than subterfuge to cover the actual design of using it in order to silence the opposition by powerfully enforcing the Sedition Act.

Historians have generally rejected this thesis. "This indictment, that the regular and provisional armies were designed primarily to suppress democracy, and not to protect the country against France," wrote Professor Morison, "is not supported by the slightest evidence." Henry Adams believed that only because no French invasion of the United States took place could Republicans assert that the standing army was designed to crush the Republican party.

Whether such an intention was foremost in the minds of such men as Hamilton, Pickering, Sedgwick, Tracy, and Cabot when they first urged the establishment of a sizable military machine it is difficult to prove, but there is con-

clusive evidence that they expected and hoped to use armed force against their political opponents.[2] The most important man in the new army of 1798-99 was Hamilton, and Hamilton was a well-known advocate of military force as the backbone of law. . . .

Hamilton's distrust of republican government and his fear that it could only end in disorder and despotism was abiding, as was his conviction that an aristocratic government was the most successful ever devised by men.

His reading of history had convinced Hamilton that disorder and rebellion were inherent in republican society and that through disorder monarchical government became established. Just after Hamilton's tragic death, Gouverneur Morris, one of the men who knew him best, described what he believed to have been Hamilton's attitude towards the army and war crisis of 1798.

"Our poor friend Hamilton bestrode his hobby to the great annoyance of his friends, and not without injury to himself. . . . He well knew that his favorite form (of government) was inadmissible, unless as the result of civil war; and I suspect that his belief in that which he called 'an approaching crisis' arose from a conviction that the kind of government most suitable in his opinion, to this extensive country, could be established in no other way." . . .

The common belief that Hamilton considered the Alien and Sedition Acts too extreme is absolutely false, and considering the fact that the largest states, particularly Virginia, were all Southern and Republican in political complexion there

---

[2] Timothy Pickering was Secretary of State; Uriah Tracy was a Federalist Representative from Connecticut; Theodore Sedgwick and George Cabot were Federalist Senators from Massachusetts.—Ed.

Is excellent reason to conclude that Hamilton contemplated the necessity of using his military machine. Civil war would certainly have followed the attempt to realize his reactionary program. . . .

While President Adams finally concluded that Hamilton's sole purpose in organizing the army was to suppress possible domestic violence, Hamilton and his friends had still other dreams—dreams of conquest scarcely less grandiose than those of the Pizzaros. In February, 1798, American Minister Rufus King informed the Secretary of State that the expected French invasion of Spain would lead to the immediate dismemberment of the Spanish colonial empire. The Venezuelan adventurer, Francisco Miranda, he pointed out, had been kept on the British payroll for just such an eventuality and was expected to lead a full-scale revolt with the assistance of the British navy. King, writing in cipher, promised to keep Pickering up to date on British plans inasmuch as the President was certain to be approached on the subject.

What King and the Hamiltonian clique conjured up was a joint Anglo-American land and naval force meant to strike at Spanish armies from Louisiana, meeting with Miranda's insurgents somewhere in Central America. So confident and enthusiastic was King that he wrote General Pinckney of the plan while the latter was waiting in southern France after the failure of the first peace commission.[3] If England fails to stop France from re-establishing her American empire, puppet republics are sure to be erected on our very doorstep, he argued. It seemed stupid, therefore, not to co-operate fully when Britain asked for help. King envisaged a new world order emerging as the result of successfully launching independent Spanish American states under the joint protection of the United States and Great Britain. Their independence, he concluded, "presents wealth and security to the U. States, and a new balance among nations." . . .

The Federalist party as a whole favored the President's recommendations for defense measures. Many openly demanded war, while most of the leaders were at least not opposed to it. Many Federalists feared and expected the outbreak of rebellion and championed an enlarged standing army as protection against the dismemberment of the Union, while behind their fears lay the desire to use force against political opposition. Again, the Federalists preferred to draw a very fine line between treason and legitimate opposition. Hamilton saw in the expected revolt an opportunity to establish the aristocratic type of government that he had always preferred and that he believed must arise out of the instability of republican societies. His dreams of military conquest and of intimate relations with Great Britain were in keeping with that order of government. His friends in the Federalist party were persuaded that a standing army for internal use had become necessary for the protection of life and property and because they preferred to interpret what they saw and heard in the Southern states as certain evidence of preparation for civil war.

Even Washington in his old age had come to look with deep concern and distrust upon the nature of the Republican opposition. Writing to Lafayette in December, 1798, he declared, "A party exists in the United States. . .which oppose the Government in all its measures, and are Clogging its Wheels indi-

---

[3] General Charles C. Pinckney was a leading South Carolina Federalist sent to negotiate a treaty with the French in 1797.—Ed.

rectly to change the nature of it, and to subvert the Constitution.''

President Adams almost alone did not share in his party's enthusiasm for the heavy military program of 1798. He had taken the lead in rousing the public to anger over French duplicity and had been the first to call for military and naval preparedness. Specifically, he had asked Congress to augment the size of the regular army, especially in the cavalry and artillery branches; he had approved the creation of a separate navy department to develop American sea power; and he had urged that American treaties with France be declared null and void. Adams did not ask for the Alien and Sedition Acts, direct taxes, new loans at high interest rates, or for a regular and provisional military force of fifty thousand men. Although none of the measures of 1798 was passed over a presidential veto, the majority in Congress broke with the President over the question of defense. By emphasizing a large army rather than a navy they put themselves into an embarrassing situation. Of what use could a large infantry force be if a French invasion did not take place?

Obviously, the seizure of Canada was out of the question, and it was not clear that Spain's North American possessions were legitimate fields of operation. By refusing to play the President's game, the dominant faction in Congress allowed their opponents to charge that the army was meant for use against American citizens. Jefferson saw his opportunity and judiciously warned his friends against giving the Federalist high command any pretext for using the newly enlarged army. He much preferred to let the public come to its own conclusions on the matter.

Hamilton, through Representative Tracy and the Secretary of War, urged the President to use his powers as Commander in Chief to direct congressional action, and when Adams refused to do so the Hamiltonians took matters into their own hands. Adams was not consulted on such vital legislation as the Sedition Act or the direct tax, and he plainly resented it. When it appeared that he had lost direction of the defense program to Hamilton and his confreres, Adams sought to obstruct their designs as consistently as Pickering and McHenry purposefully delayed in carrying out his own. . . .[4]

With an election but several months away, Adams, with the support of Wolcott, Stoddert, and the Attorney General, was still unable to end the hold that militarism had taken upon the minds of the Hamiltonians except by the most drastic action. Almost blindly the army faction refused to recognize the potency of the standing army issue in the hands of the Republicans. While Wolcott reflected the nation's changing mood his colleague, Mr. Pickering, refused to accept the warning of one of the party's most stalwart press defenders in his blunt statement that the American people did not want an army. It was in November, 1798, more than a year before the military organization was cashiered, that Noah Webster of the New York *Minerva* came out in favor of a navy rather than an army as the nation's most useful arm of defense. The die-hards such as Cabot, Ames, Pickering, and Hamilton moved stubbornly on. The army may still be useful, wrote Ames to Wolcott in answer to the latter's objections to it. Without discussing the possibility of winning the election of 1800, Ames predicted Jefferson's victory and the outbreak of civil war that would surely follow.

[4] James McHenry, Maryland Federalist, was Adams' Secretary of War.—Ed.

While doing his best to prepare the navy for what he regarded as its essential role for both defense and peace negotiations, the President gave no encouragement to the plans of the military clique. His attitude on this issue reflected a deep conviction. "The English have exhibited an amazing example of skill and intrepidity, perseverance and firmness at sea. We are a chip of that block, and we could do as we pleased, at least as we ought, on the watery element, if it were not that we shall excite jealousy in the English navy. We must, however, stand for our right."

Such was his attitude as he expressed it to his wife at the beginning of 1799. By not consulting the President on the legislation of 1798, Federalist congressional leaders had offended Adams, and by pursuing a military rather than a naval program, they had clearly angered him and opened a rift in the hitherto united ranks of the party. The act that made the split permanent, however, was the insistence on the part of Washington, Pickering, and their followers that Hamilton be made second in command. Until the President's hand was forced in favor of Hamilton, disagreement arose over issues. There was as yet no personal animosity. Adams hated Hamilton and would never have dated his commission before those of his Revolutionary friends Knox, Morgan, and Lincoln had not Washington demanded it. . . .

So far as Adams was concerned a provisional army could have been used very effectively in promoting the political strength of his own administration. Commissions would be sought and expected by many men of political importance, among them Republicans as well as Federalists. It was Adams' plan to unite the nation by commissioning outstanding Republican party leaders with the added hope that some of the more independent-minded might be won away from the Jeffersonian fold. There were men within the Republican ranks who might easily have welcomed a third political alignment between the extremes of Southern Republicanism and Eastern Hamiltonianism.

In 1805 John Adams admitted to Benjamin Rush that he had had hopes of using Madison's talents when the administration first opened but that the "ministers, whom Washington's appointment made my masters" showed open hostility to the idea. When the war scare of 1798 swept the nation Adams again sought to return to the bipartisan policy with which he had opened his administration. Like Jefferson, he recognized the middle states as holding the balance of power in national politics and attempted to woo Pennsylvania and New York Republicans with high appointments. . . .

With the election of 1800 clearly in mind Adams wrote in his diary that he had hopes of conciliating the opposition by appointing Muhlenberg and Burr to high ranks. "But I soon found myself shackled. The heads of departments were exclusive patriots. I could not name a man who was not devoted to Hamilton without kindling a fire. . . . I soon found that if I had not the previous consent of the heads of departments, and the approbation of Mr. Hamilton, I ran the utmost risk of a dead negative in the Senate." Temporary safe majorities, he concluded, made the Federalists presumptuous and vindictive.

What Adams wished to do was to appoint officers to the ranks to which their former services and revolutionary standing would entitle them. "Gates, Schuyler, Lincoln, Knox, Clintons, Pinckneys, Sumpters, Muhlenbergs, who you will. But not one of my Ministers, not one Senator, not one Representative and what was more than all, Washington who was

Viceroy over me, nor Hamilton who was Viceroy over all, would have heard the proposition with Patience. Old men with Knowledge and Experience are more worthy of Trust than Boys with their Ignorance and Vanity." . . .

Federalists not only rewarded themselves and their friends with commissions in the army, but they also believed that they were doing the nation a service in allowing politics to be the principal qualification for appointments. Our main concern, wrote Representative Goodrich of Connecticut to Oliver Wolcott, is to mind our own business abroad and "take care of our own Jacobins. . . . Some of our friends suspect a concert to get as many as they can into the army. Be that as it may, everyone of them ought to be rejected, and men only of fair property, employed in the higher and most confidential grades." Goodrich was almost liberal: his fellow Federalists were not sold on the idea of minding their own business abroad nor of appointing "Jacobins" to the lowest grades. There was general agreement, however, that the Republicans might need looking after.

The army raised in 1798 and 1799 was the principal cause of the split in the Federalist party that revealed itself blatantly when Adams suddenly announced his intention to accept the peace feelers from Paris. There can be no doubt that the party was already badly divided at the time of that startling announcement in February, 1799. In refusing to consult the President over the legislation of 1798, in changing the character of the defense measures which he had called for, in pushing Hamilton to the position of acting commander of the army, in refusing to recognize the necessity and the political expediency of giving key Republicans positions of trust in the military organization, and in the very act of

raising a large standing army the Hamiltonians had played into the hands of the Republicans and had alienated the President with his large personal following. They shortsightedly viewed the Federalist party as their factional instrument, dismissing the popularity of the President with the rank and file as of secondary importance while placing their hopes for 1800 on a civil war that Jefferson wisely cautioned his followers against giving them any pretext for starting.

The only Federalist of any significance who seemed to fully comprehend the wisdom of Adam's leadership was John Marshall. Looked upon as one of the brighter lights of the party in 1796, he was branded as a political trimmer in 1799 for his refusal to accept the French peace suggestions as false and for publicly condemning the Alien and Sedition Acts during his campaign for the House in 1798.

Marshall has "degraded himself by a mean and paltry electioneering trick," wrote Sedgwick to Pickering; and Fisher Ames went so far as to label him a "moderate" and a man who had sold himself to "the base opposers of the law." Adams offered him the seat on the Supreme Court bench left vacant by the death of James Wilson, but the Virginia Federalist preferred the active arena and accepted Washington's plea that he stand for the House of Representatives. His actions during 1799 point to him as an Adams champion and a man who saw eye to eye with the President on both domestic issues and foreign policy. Hamiltonians came to view the President's display of friendship for Marshall with almost as much alarm as his championship of Elbridge Gerry.[5]

[5] Elbridge Gerry, Massachusetts Republican, was appointed by Adams to the commission sent to negotiate a treaty with France in 1797.

Elbridge Gerry returned to the United States in the fall of 1798 as an avowed exponent of peace with France and as such was shunned by every respectable member of the Essex circle.[6] The resentment and chagrin that Adams had at first felt towards Gerry gradually softened. He had appointed him to the peace commission over the protests of his secretaries and felt their apparent triumph over him deeply. By October Gerry's social visits to the Adams home at Quincy had the local Federalist chieftains worried. It seemed to them that Gerry had somehow cast a spell over the President and that his insidious propaganda might have damaging results to the all-important Federalist war program.

Samuel Sewall was at first delegated to call upon Adams to express the anxiety of his political friends over his apparent intimacy with a Francophile, but realizing that Sewall had never been anything but hostile towards Gerry, the Essex leaders delegated newcomer Harrision Otis for the diplomatic task. It failed to impress Adams that Gerry was viewed as a suspicious character. He had known it and felt it somewhat himself before hearing the full story that Gerry had to relate. Wol-

cott, whom the Federalist leaders rightly regarded as trusted by Adams, was then instructed to inform the President how "the friends of Government" felt towards the obnoxious Mr. Gerry.

Adams could not take the warnings of Wolcott, Otis, and their friends as the basis for his actions, because he was convinced that peace could soon be arranged without humiliation to either nation and because peace was his avowed aim. The President could not avoid nominating William Vans Murray as envoy to France in February, 1799, if he was an honest man. Too many forces were at work that pointed to peace as the only sane and honorable path for him to follow. His policy, despite the machinations of the Hamiltonians, had proved successful, and for very excellent reasons he believed that peace might prove as great a political blessing in 1799 as the threat of war had been in 1797 and 1798. John Adams was a patriot, but he was also a far more astute politician than most historians have given him credit for being. When he saw an opportunity to benefit the nation and the political fortunes of John Adams he quite naturally seized upon it.

[6] A group of important Massachusetts Federalist leaders.

In the following selection, SHAW LIVERMORE (1926-   ), of the University of Michigan, attributes the decline of the Federalist party to the rejection of the basic principles of Federalism by a majority of voters. The party was committed to an elitist philosophy of government, appropriate perhaps to an earlier age but impractical in a society where democratic ideas were gaining mastery. Stubbornly clinging to their convictions, Federalists refused to modify them to gain votes. This intransigence courted political suicide and raises the question why the Federalists did not, as politicians usually do, adjust their ideology to political realities.°

► The Irrelevance of Federalist Ideas

News of peace reached New York on Saturday, the ninth of February, 1815. A grateful populace celebrated far into the night, then streamed into churches the next day to hear sermons thanking God for his rich blessings. The war was over and, for the moment, domestic quarrels gave way to profound relief. Twenty years of painfully bitter partisan jarrings between Federalists and Jeffersonian Republican. had preceded that first Sabbath of peace in almost three years. The surcease. was brief. A respected newspaper claimed on Monday that the people did not inquire about the terms of the peace, for they were "sick at heart. . .of a war that threatened to wring from them the

remaining means of subsistence, and of which they could see neither the object nor the end." The editor, William Coleman, who had been picked by Alexander Hamilton to edit the *New York Post*, thus kept aloft the tattered Federalist ensign he had helped guard through long years of defeat and frustration.

The achievements of Federalist rule under Washington and Adams had been spectacular. Just as spectacular, perhaps, was the decline of Federalist strength after the "Revolution of 1800." The presidential election that year had been a titanic one, hard tought and closely contested. Yet in 1804 the Federalist cam-

---

°Reprinted from *The Twilight of Federalism* by Shaw Livermore by permission of the Princeton University Press. Copyright © 1962 by Princeton University Press. Pages 1-15. Footnotes omitted.

°Reprinted from *The Twilight of Federalism* by Shaw Livermore by permission of the Princeton University Press. Copyright © 1962 by Princeton University Press. Pages 1-15. Footnotes omitted.

°Reprinted from *The Twilight of Federalism* by Shaw Livermore by permission of the Princeton University Press. Copyright © 1962 by Princeton University Press. Pages 1-15. Footnotes omitted.

°Reprinted from *The Twilight of Federalism* by Shaw Livermore by permission of the Princeton University Press. Copyright © 1962 by Princeton University Press. Pages 1-15. Footnotes omitted.

paign against Jefferson was as desultory as the succeeding one when Madison was first elected. Federalists, with deep misgivings, had decided in 1812 to support a dissident Republican, but the same dismal results followed. The battle of 1800 had been fought with vigor and numbers; those afterwards seemed to reflect a party hopelessly in decline and without spirit. What had happened?

To most Federalists the crisis arose from the heresies that first had overwhelmed the French monarchy and then, in their view, had become the tools of cynical American demagogues. Senseless destruction of traditional institutions like religion, government by the rich and able, agencies for preserving domestic law and order as well as for warding off foreign enemies, and accepted rules governing relations between classes—all this was to Federalists implicit in the hateful word *democracy*. The most damnable sin for a politican was flattery of the people, telling the unfit that they were able to govern themselves. It would unhinge an orderly society, and this precisely was what Federalists expected of Jeffersonianism with its intellectual freight of government by the many, free thought, and ill-concealed license. Was it not natural that the Jeffersonians would set up a cry to make suffrage open to every man whether or not he could demonstrate even a small measure of responsibility? Federalism was the creed of those nourished on the experience of colonial America or contemporary England; it grappled with and then was overwhelmed by those who understood that the nineteenth century was to be the century of democracy and individualism and that America would be its harbinger.

Federalism was the political expression of those who sought security and self-fulfillment in an ordered, structured social system. In this view, life's perils could be met only by men and women acting in concert, deriving strength from others about them and in turn lending their own talents and obedience to the whole. The very essence of civilization was a carefully wrought social fabric, a fabric that was delicate in the extreme, reflecting as it did a careful balancing of the capacities and ambitions of men on the one hand with traditions, opportunities, and dangers of the other. For survival and happiness men must recognize the hostility of nature and the power of religious precepts regarding man's sinfulness. To cope with them demanded that each person recognize his inability to face such perils alone; instead, he must do for the whole society what he could best do and accept gratefully from the whole what it believed his due. Such a conception rested upon an understanding that men's abilities were markedly diverse and that society itself was an entity separate from the individuals who composed it. This idea, of course, was an old one. Organic or anthropomorphic conceptions of society had been set forth by innumerable political philosophers since antiquity and had formed the basis for seventeenth- and eighteenth-century English society from which most Americans had come. Through the colonial period it had been the prevailing view of society though the materials for revolt from it built up steadily.

Between about 1775 and 1825 the prevailing attitude of Americans toward their society changed drastically toward the distinctive individualism which Tocqueville has described so dramatically. Jeffersonianism became the political vehicle for this change and, because a basic reorientation occurred in American society, Federalism was simply swept from the field. Never again would a major political party rest upon the old attachment to an organic society. Federalism shone forth brilliantly in the 1790's, partly because of a few dominating leaders and the remarkable acceptance of the Constitution, but its foundation as a political party, belief in an integrated, functional society, fast slipped away. It could not hope to remain a majority party however many thousands of devoted partisans remained to regret the new order of things. Jefferson's party, which had first formed as a center of opposition to certain Federalist policies, soon became the political expression of those who believed that Americans were destined to find ultimate happiness and fulfillment in themselves, in their own endeavors, and their own resources. Men were going out from society, convinced that it had stultified instead of developed, corrupted instead of ennobled. Self-reliance, fulsome dreams of men sucking out of nature its true bounty, and boundless optimism characterized these Americans who joined under Jefferson's standard. To splinter society and release the individual was their aim. America the fruitful, Americans the finders of grace within themselves—these would be the cement which bound together the new society.

Such a view helps to dispel the confusion that has come often from interpolating from its leadership the nature of the Federalist party as a party. The party's candidates were successful in hundreds of elections held on the state and local levels. These elections simply could not be won by the votes of only the rich, the well-born, and the educated, in spite of the fact that suffrage restrictions existed in most of the states. Recent scholarship has indicated that these restrictions did not confine the electorate to such a narrow basis as has been thought by some. What is more to the point is that many people did not bother to vote or they voted for men who were used to governing along accepted lines. Federalism clearly had a solid appeal that extended well below the upper ranks of society even though it is true that once Jefferson's party had made its vision of the future clear to all Americans and had effectively organized these followers, this appeal was not sufficient to form a national majority.

The functional society had deeper roots in some parts of the country than others. In general it persisted longest in areas that had been fully settled before the Revolution, areas such as Connecticut, the land of "steady habits," much of southeastern Pennsylvania, and the Valley of Virginia. Often the distinctive role of religious leaders (Connecticut) or the existence of tightly knit European communities (the Pennsylvania Dutch) reinforced this respect for a functional society. Such places were likely to have a relatively small net increase in population, usually indicating that people were emigrating but few were coming in to settle. Those who went out, unless they went in substantial groups such as certain New England settlements in Ohio, were generally attracted to the Jeffersonian party. This large-scale moving away from society thus contributed to the social disorganization that marked the 1820's and 1830's, a trend which was further hastened by industrialism with its attendant urbanization.

The characteristic Federalist understanding of political leadership lends further weight to this general view of the different bases upon which our first two major parties rested. Again and again Federalists stressed the importance of highly skilled leaders, who could be drawn from only a small segment of society. While Jeffersonians increasingly tended to emphasize rotation in office and the binding nature of instruction of U.S. senators and representatives by state legislatures, Federalists insisted upon the value of experience and independence.

The function of governing was, in the Federalist view, to be understood and practiced by the few, just as watchmaking or blacksmithing. Contrary to the general case in Europe, no narrow ruling class had emerged in the American colonies, but there had been a general acceptance of the fact that political leaders would be drawn from a distinct layer of society. Drawing from this tradition, Jefferson labored to develop a theory of a natural aristocracy, but by championing the destruction of old social forms and bonds he inexorably laid the groundwork for the familiar Jacksonian belief in government by the people, as well as of and for them. Where Federalists proudly claimed that their party was led by men of wealth and talents, Jeffersonians soon made the claim a term of derision; what warrant was there for this outmoded practice when men had now seen that they could face life's perils by themselves? One man was as good and capable as another if he but applied himself.

Even in their days of triumph and glory the Federalists had begun to suffer from a curiously enervating melancholy. The personality of Fisher Ames strikingly personified this mood. Ames was a brilliant young Federalist politician from Massachusetts who rose to leadership of Federalist forces in Congress during the late 1790's. At times he seemed to have a Rasputin-like effect upon his colleagues as he sketched violent word-pictures of Jacobins—the followers of Robespierre and Danton—rapidly turning America into a vast pest-hole. Some said the doleful prophecies of this brooding, tragic figure hung over the Federalist house forever afterward. Indeed, visions of the right-thinking being cut down by myrmidons, men seduced by claims that the few should no longer shape the destiny of the many, seemingly transfixed the Federalist psyche well before the climactic struggle of 1800. After that year it appeared that some Federalists even hoped secretly that the ignorant would soon debase society completely; then everyone could see that the prophecy had come to pass. The Federalist struggle to preserve their world was seriously compromised by a kind of death-wish, a feeling that the bell had tolled.

One also finds the cause of Federalism's decline in antiquated and inept political techniques. From the lack of systematic proselyting, to badly defined lines of command, and on to the inclinations of Federalist leaders to be prima donnas and indulge in raucous public quarrels with their comrades, the record is one of almost uniformly bad management. Federalist leaders, for the most part, seemed to assume a communion of interest among their followers and fellow leaders that did not require attention to party organization and control from legislative halls down to the humblest supporter. The indispensable organizers, the smoothers, the fixers, the disciplinarians, and the publicists were largely missing from the Federalist ranks. Jeffersonian leaders, on the other hand, used infinite finesse in carefully worded party platforms at the state and local levels, statements of principles that would appeal widely by blurring internal quarrels and striking at the enemy's weaknesses. The legislative caucus, whereby party leaders could squabble in private and then present closed ranks when voting for the record or presenting candidates for office, was quickly developed by the Jeffersonians into an unusually effective device, one that demanded a variety of ways by which secondary party leaders could be disciplined. Rarely did a Federalist leader realize that these political devices were part of a whole which could not be effected piecemeal. For Republicans they had flowed naturally from a sensitive appraisal of an electorate which increasingly rejected any notion that some men were destined to rule. Among men who had come to make political judgments for themselves, entirely new political techniques were required to develop governing majorities.

That America would survive the triumph of Jeffersonianism was of course irrelevant to Federalists whose vital years were spent glorying in the golden years before 1800 and then languishing in anger when they were swept out of national office, never to return. Federalists were extremely proud of their accomplishments. They believed they had turned the new Constitution into a viable instrument of government, secured the nation's finances, founded a sound military force, gained the respect of foreign nations, and restored confidence among the doers and builders, the men who would turn America's potential riches into real wealth. These were indeed formidable achievements in twelve years. Small wonder that Federalists gaped in disbelief when the voters shunned them to follow a man who damned so many of these policies, who announced no coherent economic, diplomatic, or defense policies of his own, and who instead talked vaguely about the glories of being a small farmer or about the general rights of man. Genuine incredulity and frustration mixed with a long-standing abhorrence of democracy-mongering generated a prodigious wrath. The Federalists, overwhelmed by despair, sullenly flung curses at their antagonists, their own number, and at the air they breathed.

Stunned by their defeat and by the manifest popularity of Jefferson, many Federalists simply lapsed into waspish parochialism. Others tried hard to blunt the developing lines of Republican policy. They vigorously opposed the purchase of Louisiana, avowedly on constitutional grounds, but most of them probably sensed that little help to Federalism

would come from this huge addition of lands in the West. Later, when Republicans refused to recharter the national bank in 1811, Federalists feared that the great fiscal structure reared by Hamilton was being wrecked. Few seemed aware how little Federalist legislation was actually swept away in these years. Most of the time the major issue was the Republican embargo policy. While opposing military intervention in the Napoleonic wars, Federalists insisted that American merchants and seamen had a right to trade with whomever they wished. The government, in their view, was bound to protect that commerce by diplomatic and, if necessary, military means, rather than by forbidding American ships and goods to leave the country. Above all, Federalists demanded that a more powerful military and naval establishment be set up at once.

After three years of intricate twistings, the Madison administration finally chose war. Federalists as a body had contested this path, and they continued to condemn the war after it had begun. As military defeats followed one upon the other and the public debt began to swell, Federalists sharpened their attacks upon Madison and his political friends. Because few Americans had more than a fuzzy idea how the war had come about or what would be gained by it, grumbling increased in many areas, countered only in part by sentiments of inchoate patriotism. Federalists smelled political gains; indeed at the fall elections in 1814 they suddenly broke their skein of political losses and made sharp advances. More than a third of the members of both houses in the next Congress would be Federalists. All of the New England states were safely in their hands, together with Maryland and Delaware. Federalists elected a third of New York's lower house, had just short of a majority in New Jersey's legislature and about 30 per cent of Pennsylvania's two houses. The solid bank of Republicans in Pennsylvania's congressional delegation was broken up by the election of five Federalists. Outside the New England and middle states, however, Federalist prospects did not brighten noticeably. "Mr. Madison's War" was still generally popular in the South and West, in spite of lively Federalist minorities in Virginia and the Carolinas. Some Federalist newspapers were still published in Kentucky and Ohio, but their readers were few in number.

Federalist dreams of a continuing resurgence were shattered, however, by three events that followed hard upon each other. The infamous Hartford Convention met on December 15, 1814, the peace treaty at Ghent was signed Christmas eve, and General Jackson's army leveled Pakenham's forces at New Orleans on January 8. Accumulated vexations, perhaps topped by a marauding British expedition sent to the Maine coast, prompted New England Federalist leaders to meet in Hartford during the bleakest hours of the war for the purpose of agreeing upon formal grievances and remedies to be tendered the national government. Although relative moderates controlled the convention, the circumstances, together with the long list of demands that touched the fundamental nature of the union, convinced many that the delegates were threatening secession. Such a threat made during war was easily equated with treason. Federalist leaders and editors strove to allay such fears, but at the same time a majority of Federalists in New England and the middle states appear to have believed that the convention's proposals were good ones, and, above all, that the delegates had a perfect right to meet and petition the federal government. Within a few weeks, however, it was clear that the political effects were

crushing. Republican spokesmen quickly made the convention an opprobrious epithet that was good currency for years. Embittered Federalists never could appreciate the exquisite irony in the fact that the convention's report was made many days after the peace treaty was signed, but before news of it reached America. . . .

Although changes had occurred during the war itself, the first comprehensive statement of a new Republican direction came with President Madison's recommendations that accompanied the peace treaty he submitted to the Senate in February. Foremost among them was a request for the maintenance of an adequate regular military and naval force in peacetime. Further, he asked that Congress take suitable measures for proper harbor defense, for the cultivation of the military art, and for adding a measure of discipline to the "distinguished bravery" of the militia. Madison did not stop there. He also suggested a system of direct internal taxation, advocated higher salaries for public officers, and made an eloquent appeal for assistance to manufacturers. Madison's firm sponsorship of a new national bank drew special attention from Federalist observers. The rancorous Republican opposition to rechartering the first bank in 1811 was still fresh in their minds when administration leaders proposed a second bank in the 1814-15 session. Bickering over details killed it then, but the proposal was quickly revived. A Federalist wag described the turn of events thus: "They are now, good souls, heartily in love with a national bank. A lover never sighed half so much for his absent fair-one, as they have within the year for the establishment of a bank." Most of Madison's proposals, of course, were good Federalist doctrine for which the originators had been relentlessly attacked in recent years. . . .

NOBLE E. CUNNINGHAM, JR. (1926-   ), of the University of Missouri, explores the way Republicans once in power turned a two-party system into a one-party system. By examining the sources of Republican supremacy, Cunningham helps to account for Federalist decline. He maintains that the Republicans built a strong party organization and elaborated doctrines and pursued policies which made them the dominant party nationally. As a party born in opposition in the 1790s, the Republicans by necessity had to develop techniques and formulate programs that would attract votes. The Republicans were so successful that the first American two-party system did not survive. The following selection comes from a two-volume study of the development of Republican party organization during the years 1789 to 1809.°

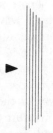

The Sources of
Republican Supremacy

Nearly a thousand persons packed the old semicircular Senate chamber in the unfinished Capitol on March 4, 1801. Senators, representatives, and others fortunate enough to crowd into the room strained to hear the President's inaugural address delivered in a barely audible tone, and they watched intently as Chief Justice John Marshall administered the oath of office to Thomas Jefferson as the third President of the United States. "I have this morning witnessed one of the most interesting scenes, a free people can ever witness," declared a thoughtful observer. "The changes of administration, which in every government and in every age have

most generally been epochs of confusion, villainy and bloodshed, in this our happy country take place without any species of distraction, or disorder. The scene which Mrs. Samuel Harrison Smith, wife of the editor of the Washington *National Intelligencer*, thus appreciatively witnessed has been so periodically repeated in American history as to make the inheritors of this enduring political system unmindful of the great importance of the events of March 4, 1801. What occurred on that day was far more than the first inaugural ceremony in the new capital at Washington. It was the first time in the nation's history that political power in the

°Reprinted from *The Jeffersonian Republicans in Power* by Noble E. Cunningham, Jr., by permission of the University of North Carolina Press. Copyright © 1963 by the University of North Carolina Press. Pages 1-11, 300-305. Footnotes omitted.

national government was transferred from one political party to another.

That such a change should take place without incident seems less eventful today to Americans, conditioned by the history of an uninterrupted pattern of such political behavior, than to contemporaries, who two weeks before the inauguration had feared the disastrous consequences of the House of Representatives failing to decide the electoral tie between Jefferson and Aaron Burr. Although the election of 1800 had clearly demonstrated the nation's wish that Jefferson should be president, the verdict of the electorate was threatened when the tie vote threw the election into the House. There, until the new Congress convened, the Federalists had a majority. Nearly a week of voting and thirty-five ballots produced no decision; it was conceivable that such a deadlock could continue through March 4, when President John Adam's term came to an end. What then would have been the consequences? Fortunately for the future of the American political system this question did not have to be faced; on February 17, on the thirty-sixth ballot, Jefferson, receiving the votes of ten of the sixteen states, was elected.

Thus on March 4 the executive branch passed without disruption from Federalist to Republican control. Since President John Adams had retained all of President Washington's Cabinet when he took office in 1797, Jefferson's appointment of a new Cabinet was to mark the first time that a complete change in the executive department had occurred. The most important Cabinet posts went to men prominent in Republican leadership and in service to the party. The President's close political confidant James Madison, who had played a major role in the formation of the Republican party, became Secretary of State. Pennsylvania's Albert Gallatin, who had recently headed the Republican leadership in Congress, received the Treasury post. The appointment of two leading Massachusetts Republicans—Henry Dearborn as Secretary of War and Levi Lincoln as Attorney General—emphasized the national basis of the party. Another New England Republican, Gideon Granger of Connecticut, was named Postmaster General, an office of influence though not of Cabinet rank. After considerable difficulty in obtaining a Secretary of the Navy, Jefferson settled on Robert Smith of Maryland, brother of Congressman Samuel Smith, to complete his official family. In the new Seventh Congress, a Republican majority in both the House and the Senate was to replace what had previously been a Federalist majority in both houses. In both executive and legislative branches, the transfer of political power, so significant for the future of the American party system, was thus complete.

The political parties which participated in this party changeover were of even more recent origin than the national government installed only twelve years before. Although George Washington had begun his presidency in 1789 under nonparty conditions, two parties were fairly distinctly formed by the time he left office in 1797. In the presidential election of 1796, Federalist John Adams and Republican Thomas Jefferson faced each other in the nation's first party contest for the presidency, and the campaign left little doubt that the political groupings which had emerged under the new government had assumed the definite character of political parties. The clearcut party conditions created by the results of this election—the inauguration of a Federalist president and the convening of a Federalist-controlled Congress—speeded the party system toward maturity. As the opposition party the Republicans, in resorting to extensive organizational and electioneering efforts to turn the Federalists out of office, contributed markedly to the development and to the permanency of the party system. The Republicans and the Federalists who faced each other in the vigorous political campaign of 1800 displayed a degree of organization, party discipline, and effective campaign methods largely unknown a decade before. Although a system of political parties had not come to be accepted in theory and neither party recognized the validity nor usefulness of its opponent, in practice the operation of parties had become an essential feature of the nation's political life. . . .

The victory which Republicans so enthusiastically hailed in 1801 was basically a party triumph. The election of Jefferson and of a Republican Congress had been accomplished through four years of party organizing, vigorous political campaigning, and realistic fashioning of party machinery, made effective by the ability of the Republican party to sense and to conform to the temper of the electorate. In the post-mortems held by Federalists following their fall from power, Federalist leaders privately credited Republican success to superior party organization and methods, and, though professing to abhor Republican methods, they sought to imitate their rivals. "I hope it is not too late to wrench the name *republican* from those who have unworthily usurped it. . .," wrote Fisher Ames, early in 1801. "Names and appearances are in party warfare arms and ammunition. It is particularly necessary to contest this name with them now." The new administration "must not begin with an impression on the popular mind that we are a disgraced if we are a disappointed party. We must court popular favor, we must study public

opinion, and accommodate measures to what it is and still more to what it ought to be." Delaware's James A. Bayard, discussing Federalist policy with Alexander Hamilton, similarly suggested: "We shall probably pay more attention to public opinion than we have heretofore done, and take more pains, not merely to do right things, but to do them in an acceptable manner." Hamilton, replying with a proposal for an extensive organization of the Federalist party, agreed that Federalists had "erred in relying so much on the rectitude and utility of their measures as to have neglected the cultivation of popular favor, by fair and justifiable expedients. . . . Unluckily, however, for us, in the competition for the passions of the people, our opponents have great advantages over us. . . .unless we can contrive to take hold of, and carry along with us some strong feelings of the mind, we shall in vain calculate upon any substantial or durable results. Although Federalists overstated the case in contrasting their own reliance on principles to the Republican appeals to passion, the Republican party had taken the initiative in organizing party machinery, providing for popular participation in party affairs, and effectively presenting the party's program and its candidates to the electorate.

The Federalist party never recovered from its defeat in the election of 1800 and was never to return to power in the national government, but it did continue to maintain sizable support in some areas; and there was always an active Federalist opposition in Congress throughout Jefferson's two terms. New England Federalists remained most loyal to their party; one state, Connecticut, remained Federalist throughout Jefferson's presidency. There were important Federalist minorities in New York, Pennsylvania, New Jersey, and Maryland; Delaware, although partially recruited into the Republican camp in 1801 and 1802, returned to Federalism in 1804. The Federalists were also supported by a powerful press. Overwhelming Republican strength in some areas and a strong majority in Congress made Republicans at times careless of party unity, but Republican leaders never discounted the possibility of a Federalist resurgence. The likelihood of the Federalists profiting from Republican divisions was, in fact, realistically feared. . . .

Jefferson in his inaugural address voiced a hope for the reconciliation of parties, and at the beginning of his administration he made some steps in that direction. "The people have come over in a body to the republican side, and have left such of their leaders as were incurable to stand by themselves," he wrote shortly after his inauguration, "so that there is every reason to hope that that line of party division which we saw drawn here, will be totally obliterated." That Jefferson, like most of his contemporaries, did not fully appreciate the party system which he was helping to establish was reflected in other letters, written soon after taking office, in which he hopefully anticipated the end of political parties. "The symptoms of a coalition of parties give me infinite pleasure," he wrote, March 22, 1801. "Setting aside only a few only, I have been ever persuaded that the great bulk of both parties had the same principles fundamentally, and that it was only as to our foreign relations there was any division. These I hope can be so managed as to cease to be a subject of division for us. Nothing shall be spared on my part to obliterate the traces of party and consolidate the nation, if it can be done without abandonment of principle." But the consolidation of parties did not take place, and Jefferson early abandoned his hopes of reconciling the Federalists.

"The attempt at reconciliation was honourably pursued by us for a year or two and spurned by them," he later explained. In fact, as early as December 1802 he confessed that "instead of conciliation their bitterness is got to that excess which forbids further attention to them." Jefferson was to leave the presidency with no more amity toward, nor from, the Federalists than when he had taken office.

The Federalists in the presidential election of 1804 made no national contest, and Jefferson's sweeping victory of 162 electoral votes to 14 for Charles Cotesworth Pinckney appeared to foretell the doom of the Federalist party. Jefferson in 1807 affirmed his belief that the Federalists were "compleately vanquished, and never more to take the field under their own banners. They will now reserve themselves to profit by the schisms among republicans." But that the Federalist party had not disappeared was soon demonstrated in the presidential election of 1808. Federalist candidate Charles Cotesworth Pinckney carried all of New England, except Vermont, and also won Delaware, two of Maryland's eleven votes, and three of North Carolina's fourteen electoral votes. James Madison's 122 electoral votes represented a substantial victory over Pinckney's 47 electoral votes, but the Federalist party could by no means be dismissed from the political scene. Although the party conflict during Jefferson's administration was an unequal contest, the majority party was never without significant active or potential opposition from the Federalist minority.

As he took the oath of office on March 4, 1801, Jefferson could have little anticipated the problems which would most occupy the attention of his administration. His inaugural address, devoted almost exclusively to the domestic scene, referred briefly to foreign policy, where he was to accomplish his greatest success, the purchase of Louisiana, and experience his greatest disappointment, the failure of the Embargo. His immediate goal was to put into operation the program which he and his party had promised in the election of 1800: a policy of retrenchment or, in Jeffersonian terms, "simplicity and frugality." In the opening years of his administration, a Republican majority in both houses of Congress enacted the President's program, demonstrating the maturity of the party system by this revision of public policy through the party process. In his first message to Congress in December 1801, Jefferson recommended the abolition of all internal taxes, reductions in the army, navy, and civil government, and announced the steps which had already been taken to reduce officers under executive authority. Philip Norborne Nicholas, chairman of the Virginia Republican General Committee, rejoiced: "The presidents communication to congress has met the warmest approbation of the Republicans here both on account of the manner and the matter. The idea of such a diminution of the taxes will secure to the administration the hearts of the people more than any thing which could happen. This is an argument which will have weight in every part of the Union and with all parties." Delaware's Caesar A. Rodney agreed: "The message of the President must have a wonderful effect on the Country. Nothing can be better calculated to answer the public expectation at this important period. . . . When the people find Mr. Jefferson in his first communication to congress recommending the abolition of all internal taxation—of the 'odious stamp act,' of the excise 'the horror of all free states,' of the carriage tax . . . they will

look up to him as the 'Father of the Commonwealth.' "

Federalists generally opposed the Jeffersonian program and constantly complained of too many changes for the sake of change, as Connecticut Congressman Roger Griswold cynically protested in December 1801:

Under this administration nothing is to remain as it was. Every minutia is to be changed. When Mr. Adams was President, the door of the president's House opened to the East. Mr. Jefferson has closed that door and opened a new door to the West. General Washington and Mr. Adams opened every Session of Congress with a speech. Mr. Jefferson delivers no speech, but makes his communication by a written message. I fear that you Aristocrats of New England will think these important changes unnecessary and be apt to say that they are made with a view only to change, but you ought to recollect that you are neither Philosophers or skilled in the mysteries of Democratic policy.

The incoming Republican administration, however, was faced with a new set of political circumstances that called for more fundamental changes in policy and in strategy than those deplored by Griswold. The Republican party now found itself under vastly changed conditions; no longer the opposition party but the party in power, its future success rested on its ability to function and prosper under the pressures of national responsibility. Would the cement supplied by common opposition to the Federalist regime now dissolve? How would the party act in regard to such practical political problems as the patronage? How could party supremacy be maintained? The Jeffersonian Republican party, which through the successful operation of practical political machinery and well-developed party methods had turned the Federalists out of office, was now faced with the equally challenging problem of staying in power.

As the development of the Republican party entered a new and significant phase, Jefferson and his party lieutenants did not overlook the importance of completing party organization in states where it was still incomplete, nor did they underestimate the need to utilize political patronage for party purposes, yet at the same time neither did the party leaders lose sight of the necessity to keep the Republican party attuned to the hopes and the needs of the American people. . . .

The functioning of the party as a political mechanism during these years in office revealed a close attention to party organization and methods, a utilization of the power of the press and of the patronage, and a deference to the ultimate power of the voter. The Jeffersonians exhibited a thoroughly realistic organization aimed at maintaining the support of the electorate and perpetuating the political power of the party. The institutions, mechanisms, and methods directed to this end were remarkably successful, yet it remains clear that these would have been unavailing had not the party pursued the policies and produced the leaders that conformed to the temper of the nation. Conversely, the aspirations of the electorate might never have found effective implementation without the device of party.

The party which Jefferson turned over to Madison's guidance was, as it had been since its formation, a national party held together by the goal of controlling the national administration through which its programs and interests could be translated into action. The party members in Congress continued, as they had since the beginning, to form the basic national party organization, assisted under conditions of power by the party leaders in the executive branch. The nominating caucus, though still challenged as it had been since its first usage, established by repeated performance its control over the party's nominations for president and vice-president. As a national party, the Republican structure was, however, always dependent upon its component parts in the states, and its national strength and unity were severely strained by the local party schisms which had broken out once the party was firmly in power. State and local issues and little-known personalities always affected the sum total of the party's success.

While the national party machinery remained little altered during Jefferson's years in office, state party organizations, reflecting the varying conditions and issues of the federated union, exhibited a variety of growth and activity. Yet, although the party organization within the various states differed in many details, there are certain patterns of party development which stand out when the two decades before 1809 are viewed as a whole. The development of formal party machinery was plainly influenced by the extent of party conflict. Party organization developed most rapidly in those states which were most closely divided between Republicans and Federalists. Thus in the period before Jefferson's election, the closest contest between Republicans and Federalists had occurred in the middle states, especially New York and Pennsylvania, and including also New Jersey in 1800. Party organization in these states by 1800 was the most advanced and extensive in the nation. During the period of Jefferson's presidency, the most extensive party organizational efforts took place in the New England states, where Republicans were more vigorously challenged by the Federalists than anywhere in the country.

The development of party machinery was also directly influenced by state electoral procedures, particularly the presence or absence of statewide elections. The demands of waging state-wide political campaigns produced state-wide organizations which otherwise would not have been deemed necessary. The states which exhibited the least amount of formal party machinery, principally the states south of Virginia and in the West, either displayed little party conflict or lacked state-wide elections. When there were neither state-wide elections nor substantial party opposition, party organization remained largely informal.

The first party organizations of the 1790's centered primarily in the hands of political leaders and influential local citizens; a state party caucus of members of the legislature and other party leaders commonly exercised the decisive voice in state nominations and the affairs of the party in the state. Early machinery generally was initiated by party leaders and tended to develop from the top down. This was largely true of party organization before 1800, and the same pattern continued after 1800 in most states where formal party machinery was then being initially introduced. In the years from 1801 to 1809, the New England states went through the initial stage of erecting party machinery on an extensive scale. Most of this organization came from the top down: it was commonly headed by a legislative caucus; the state committees tended to dominate the state organization and to pass instructions down to the county and local committees. In Connecticut the state party manager had unusually wide powers. What took place in the New England states in these years was basically what had taken place in states such as New York and Pennsylvania in the previous decade. There state party cau-

cuses, state committees, and centralized control from influential party leaders had set the pattern for party organization and largely determined the operations of the party. Differences in details of party structure were many, but the general pattern was similar.

Once party machinery was established and regularized procedures adopted for making party nominations and conducting party campaigns, these procedures, by the nature of the political process, directly involved not only party leaders but also ordinary voters. As the voter became more active politically and more familiar with the operations of the party, his role became increasingly important in party procedures. Party leaders in the early stages of party development frequently organized public participation, much of which was so completely directed from the top down as to afford very superficial popular participation. However, this activity, though guided, controlled, and used to advance the decisions of the party leaders, accustomed the voters to taking part in party affairs. This participation and experience in party matters tended to produce within states in which party machinery was well developed a trend toward more democratic procedures within the party. Thus a pattern of increasing intra-party popular participation emerged.

When Jefferson returned to Monticello in March 1809, he ended nearly two decades of active participation in national political life, broken only by three years of retirement, from 1794 to 1797. In these formative years of the American party system no man stood longer in the center of political activity than Jefferson. Although in the early development of the Republican party Madison more than Jefferson had been the party organizer, it was Jefferson who emerged as the chief party leader and the symbol of the aspirations of the Republican interest. It was Jefferson who inspired and led the mobilization of the Republican party which turned the Adams Federalists out of power in 1800, and it was Jefferson who guided the party under the initial critical test of holding the reins of power.

Jefferson in 1798 wrote that "in every free and deliberating society there must, from the nature of man, be opposite parties and violent dissensions and discords; and one of these, for the most part, must prevail over the other for a longer or shorter time. Perhaps this party division is necessary to induce each to watch and delate to the people the proceedings of the other." Despite the advanced conception of parties that can be inferred from this statement, it is not at all clear that Jefferson thought in terms of a permanent party system such as developed in the United States. He never recognized the validity of the Federalist party either while Adams was in office or as an opposition party during his own administration. His initial efforts to consolidate the two parties, though soon abandoned, appear genuine. There is every reason to believe that Jefferson was sincere when he said: "We are all republicans—we are all federalists." But the party system had become more permanent by 1801 than Jefferson himself realized.

If Jefferson, like most of his contemporaries, may not have clearly foreseen the American party system as it was to develop, he was far from naïve about the realities of politics of his own day. He clearly recognized the usefulness of party devices to advance and implement the aims of the Republican interest which he conceived of as representing the aspirations of a majority of the American people—a verdict confirmed by the election of 1800 and reaffirmed in 1804 and 1808. Although Jefferson would have been among the first to admit the importance and usefulness of party machinery, he would never have suggested that party organization and campaign methods alone would determine the outcome of any political contest; rather, he would have stressed the party's ability to express and implement the aims and the interests of the majority.

As President, Jefferson clearly demonstrated the abilities of an effective politician. He well understood the nature of a national political party which reflected regional differences, diverse interests, and clashing personalities. His ability to hold the Republican party together nationally when it was rocked by state party divisions and to retain the attachment of virtually all sides involved in the internal divisions of state politics was an accomplishment that only a superb politician could achieve. His patient toleration of party schisms on the state level reflected a realistic comprehension of local politics. His success in preventing the Randolph schism from spreading into a crippling disruption of the party nationally likewise revealed his understanding of the importance of a strong national party organization in support of his administration. Jefferson's efforts to develop a workable relationship with a party floor leader in Congress spoke clearly of his practical political sense. His close relationship with the Republican party press revealed his appreciation of that instrument for party purposes; at the same time, it indicated his basic commitment to an informed public opinion as the strength of democratic government. That Jefferson fully realized the power of party patronage and did not hesitate to use it for party advantage was demonstrated, but that he also realized the responsibilities of using that power was evident. His patronage policy, which was neither moderate enough to suit some nor sweeping enough to please many, was to a large extent the result of his efforts to balance the conflicting pressures which he felt as the leader of a national party with the broad interests of the nation.

Although Jefferson recognized his position as the head of the Republican party, he never acted as if that place gave him the commanding voice in party affairs. His party leadership was always exercised through persuasion rather than by dictation. He was invariably accessible to party leaders throughout the nation, but he never attempted to dictate to them nor to plan and manage their local party machinery. Although his sympathies in regard to state Republican schisms were sometimes evident, or confidentially revealed, he never publicly threw the weight of his party leadership nor that of the presidential office into local party disputes.

Under Jefferson the Republican party proved the workability of the party system and demonstrated the procedures for changing national policy through the operation of parties. In presenting the voters with meaningful alternatives and in implementing the electorate's decision through governmental action, the party established its utility and validity.

When Jefferson turned over the presidential office to Madison on March 4, 1809, there was proof that the Republican party had survived test of power. In so doing, the party had done much to engrain into American political life the party system, to make party government acceptable, to make party machinery a normal part of political activity, to make part and patronage inseparable, and to make the voter more conscious of political action and more active in party affairs. Jefferson retired to Monticello carrying with him the memories of the bitter rivalries with Hamilton, Adams, and other Federalist leaders, deeply scarred by the violent personal attacks made upon him by the Federalist opposition, and disappointed by his own failure to reconcile the Federalists to his administration. But more important than such outward manifestations of the party conflict through which Jefferson had moved for nearly two decades was the development of the party system which was to endure as a vital part of the American heritage.

Suggestions for Further Reading

The modern debate over the origins of American political parties stems from the seminal writings of Charles A. Beard. Shortly after he wrote *An Economic Interpretation of the Constitution* (New York, 1913), Beard published a detailed study of politics in the years after the adoption of the federal constitution entitled *The Economic Origins of Jeffersonian Democracy* (New York, 1915). For a long time Beard's views were widely accepted though some of the details were revised by Manning J. Dauer in *The Adams Federalists* (Baltimore, Md., 1953). John C. Miller, *The Federalist Era, 1789-1801* (New York, 1960) is a modern synthetic treatment of the decade. Joseph Charles, *The Origins of the American Party System* (Williamsburg, Va., 1956) is the fragment of an uncompleted larger work, yet it is full of fresh insight while retaining much of the Beardian framework. A new revisionist study of Federalists in defeat is David Fischer, *The Revolution of American Conservatism* (New York, 1965).

The growing controversy over party origins stems partly from the different perspectives social scientists other than historians bring to the problem. Among the most important examples of work by political scientists are M. Ostrogorski, *Democracy and the Organization of Political Parties* (New York, 1902), now available in an abridged paperback edition and Joseph La Palombara and Myron Weiner, eds., *Political Parties and Political Development* (Princeton, N.J., 1966). Seymour M. Lipset, *The First New Nation* (New York, 1963) is written by a sociologist.

Because the states were as important as centers of political life as the national capital, generalizations about politics must rest in part on local developments. Among the useful studies for New England are: William A. Robinson, *Jeffersonian Democracy in New England* (New Haven, Conn., 1916); Richard Purcell, *Connecticut in Transition* (Washington, 1918); Anson E. Morse, *The*

Federalist Party in Massachusetts to the Year 1800 (Princeton, N.J., 1909); and David Fischer's re-examination of Federalist leadership, "The Myth of the Essex Junto," *William and Mary Quarterly*, XXI (April, 1962), 191-235. Southern politics have been explored by John H. Wolfe, *Jeffersonian Democracy in South Carolina* (Chapel Hill, N.C., 1940) and Delbert H. Gilpatrick, *Jeffersonian Democracy in North Carolina, 1789-1816* (New York, 1931). These volumes are full of suggestive data as are two modern studies of Pennsylvania politics, Harry M. Tinkcom, *The Republicans and Federalists in Pennsylvania, 1790-1801: A Study in National Stimulus and Local Response* (Harrisburg, Pa., 1950) and Sanford W. Higginbotham, *The Keystone in the Democratic Arch: Pennsylvania Politics, 1800-1816* (Harrisburg, Pa., 1952). Two recent state studies which challenge Beard on various grounds are Harry Ammon, "The Jeffersonian Republicans in Virginia: An Interpretation," *Virginia Magazine of History and Biography*, LXXI (April, 1963), 153-167 and Alfred Young, "The Mechanics and the Jeffersonians: New York, 1789-1801," *Labor History* (Fall, 1964), 247-276.

One of the best sources of insight into politics in the early years of the Republic and the ideas and motives of party leaders are the many biographies in which this period is especially rich. Federalist leaders have been studied by John C. Miller, *Alexander Hamilton, Portrait in Paradox* (New York, 1959); Broadus Mitchell, *Alexander Hamilton: The National Adventure, 1788-1804* (New York, 1962); Cecilia Kenyon, "Alexander Hamilton: Rousseau of the Right," *Political Science Quarterly*, LXXIII (June, 1958), 161-178; Samuel E. Morison, *The Life and Letters of Harrison G. Otis, Federalist* (2 vols.; Boston, 1913); and John A. Carroll and Mary W. Ashworth, *George Washington, First in Peace* (New York, 1957). Lynn Turner, *William Plummer of New Hampshire, 1759-1850*

(Chapel Hill, N.C., 1962) is the best study of New Hampshire politics and an important examination of a Federalist who turned Republican. Samuel F. Bemis, *John Quincy Adams and the Foundations of American Foreign Policy* (New York, 1949) is an outstanding biography of another leading figure who also deserted federalism. For studies of John Adams, see Page Smith, *John Adams* (New York, 1962), and John R. Howe, Jr., *The Changing Political Thought of John Adams* (Princeton, N.J., 1966).

Among the useful biographies of Jeffersonian Republicans are: Dumas Malone, *Jefferson and the Rights of Man* (Boston, 1951) and *Thomas Jefferson and the Ordeal of Liberty* (Boston, 1962); Irving Brant, *James Madison, Father of the Constitution, 1787-1800* (New York, 1950) and *James Madison, Secretary of State, 1800-1809* (New York, 1953); Raymond Walters, *Albert Gallatin: Jeffersonian Financier and Diplomat* (New York, 1957); Henry H. Simms, *Life of John Taylor* (Richmond, 1932); and Henry Adams, *John Randolph* (New York, 1899).

Studies of the major political issues of the 1790s form another body of literature. E. James Ferguson, *The Power of the Purse* (Chapel Hill, N.C., 1961) critically re-examines Hamilton's financial program. Leland D. Baldwin, *Whiskey Rebels: The Story of a Frontier Uprising* (Pittsburgh, 1939) probes in depth domestic opposition to Hamilton's tax program.

Foreign affairs in the 1790s have been examined suggestively and imaginatively by Felix Gilbert, *To the Farewell Address* (Princeton, N.J., 1961). Basic but more traditional studies of the diplomatic history are: Samuel F. Bemis, *Jay's Treaty: A Study in Commerce and Diplomacy* (New York, 1923) and *Pinckney's Treaty: A Study of America's Advantage from Europe's Distress, 1783-1800* (New Haven, Conn., 1960); Alexander DeConde, *Entangling Alliance: Politics and Diplomacy under George Washington* (Durham, N.C., 1958); and Bradford Perkins, *The First Rapprochement: England and the United States* (Philadelphia, 1953). Paul Varg, *Foreign Policies of the Founding Fathers* (East Lansing Mich., 1963) stresses the link

between foreign affairs and domestic politics as does Joseph Charles, *The Origins of the American Party System* (Williamsburg, Va., 1956).

The impact of the French Revolution on American politics has been examined by Charles D. Hazen, *Contemporary American Opinion of the French* (Baltimore, Md., 1897); Eugene P. Link, *The Democratic-Republican Societies, 1790-1809* (New York, 1942); Marshall Smelser, "The Federalist Period as an Age of Passion," *American Quarterly*, X (1958), 391-419 and "The Jacobin Phrenzy: The Menace of Monarchism, Plutocracy and Anglophilia," *Review of Politics*, XXI (January, 1959), 239-258. See also James M. Smith, *Freedom's Fetters: The Alien and Sedition Laws and American Civil Liberties* (Ithaca, N.Y., 1956).

The growth of political organization is treated in an older book by George D. Luetscher, *Early Political Machinery in the United States* (Philadelphia, 1903), but the outstanding studies are two volumes by Noble Cunningham, Jr., *The Jeffersonian Republicans: The Formation of Party Organization, 1789-1801* (Chapel Hill, N.C., 1957) and *The Jeffersonian Republicans in Power, Party Operations, 1801-1809* (Chapel Hill, N.C., 1963).

The history of the suffrage has been restudied by Chilton Williamson, *American Suffrage, From Property to Democracy* (Princeton, N.J., 1960); Richard McCormick, *The History of Voting in New Jersey* (New Brunswick, N.J., 1953); and J. R. Pole, *Political Representation in England and the Origins of the American Republic*, (New York, 1966).

The period when the early party system declined is examined in Henry Adams' classic *History of the United States of America during the Administrations of Jefferson and Madison* (9 vols.; New York, 1889-1891) and in George Dangerfield, *The Era of Good Feelings* (New York, 1952). Charles Snydor describes some of the consequences of party decline without accounting for it in "The One-Party Period of American History," *American Historical Review*, LI (April, 1946), 439-451.